07/17

ANIMALS &
ETHICS 101:
Thinking Critically
About Animal Rights

NATHAN NOBIS

ISBN: 0692471286
ISBN-13: 978-0692471289

PREFACE

The contents of this book are based on from materials I developed to teach a course called "Animals and Ethics" for the Humane Society of the United States' *Humane Society University* from 2008-2015. Some of the course's description and goals are on the next pages. I hope these materials will find use in courses and discussion groups and be helpful for individual readers. The Humane Society University is no longer operating, but I am grateful to them for the opportunity to develop and teach this course and for the students who took part in the course.

This book can serve as a brief guide and companion to some important in-print books on animals and ethics by Peter Singer (*Animal Liberation*, among others), Tom Regan (*Empty Cages*, among others) and Mark Rowlands (*Animals Like Us*, among others) and others. This book refers to many sources, both in print and online. For online sources, I usually – but not always – provide a URL for the source; if not, I write (Google) after the source. If the given URL does not work, readers should Google the author and title (or the title in quotes) to try to find the source. Since URLs come and go and uploaded materials change, perhaps this will yield the reading. Also, who knows what other interesting sources and discussion on these issues that Google might turn up!

Please feel free to contact me with any reactions to these materials and with any suggestions or questions. I look forward to hearing from you!

Nathan Nobis, Ph.D.
Morehouse College, Atlanta, GA USA
Nathan.Nobis@Gmail.com
www.NathanNobis.com

iv

ABOUT THIS BOOK

This book provides an overview of the current debates about the nature and extent of our moral obligations to animals. Which, if any, uses of animals are morally wrong, which are morally permissible (i.e., not wrong) and *why*? What, if any, moral obligations do we, individually and as a society (and a global community), have towards animals and *why*? How should animals be treated? *Why*?

We will explore the most influential and *most developed* answers to these questions – given by philosophers, scientists, and animal advocates and their critics – to try to determine which positions are supported by the best moral reasons. Topics include:

- general theories of ethics and their implications for animals,
- moral argument analysis,
- general theories of our moral relations to animals,
- animal minds, and
- the uses of animals for food, clothing, experimentation, entertainment, hunting, as companions or pets, and other purposes.

The book offers discussion questions and paper assignments to encourage readers to develop positions on theoretical and practice issues concerning ethics and animals, give reasons for their support, and respond to possible objections and criticisms.

This book is organized around an initial presentation of three of the most influential methods of moral thinking for *human to human* interactions. We then see how these ethical theories have been extended to apply to *human to animal* interactions, i.e., how humans ought to treat non-human animals.

These perspectives are:

- a demand for equality or *equal moral consideration of interests* (developed by Peter Singer);

- a demand for respect of *the moral right to respectful treatment* (developed by Tom Regan); and
- a demand that moral decisions be made *fairly and impartially* and the use of a novel thought experiment designed to ensure this (developed by Mark Rowlands, following John Rawls).

We will see what these moral theories imply for the general "moral status" of various kinds of animals and for particular uses of animals, e.g., for food, fashion, experimentation, entertainment, and other purposes. We attempt to evaluate these theories as true or false, well-supported or not and the arguments based on them as sound or unsound.

We will also survey general moral theories that imply that we have few if any, moral obligations to animals and other arguments given in defense of various uses of animals. One challenge for learning about ethics and animals is that there are fewer defenses of harmful animal use *developed by professional ethicists* than critiques of animal use. Since the common view is that animal use does not raise serious moral issues, perhaps people often do not see much need to defend that assumption. Nevertheless, we will find materials that provide the strongest and most common defenses of various uses of animals so that we might evaluate the arguments in favor of these positions.

PRIMARY READINGS

The theories from Singer, Regan and Rowlands are developed in these books, and others:

1. Peter Singer, *Animal Liberation*, 3rd Edition (Ecco 2002, 1990, 1975). http://www.princeton.edu/~psinger/

   A classic, the book that started the modern animal protection movement.

2. Tom Regan, *Empty Cages: Facing the Challenge of Animal Rights* (Rowman & Littlefield, 2004). http://tomregan-animalrights.com

   A descendent of a classic, Tom Regan's 1983 *The Case for Animal Rights*. In addition to an argument that many animals possess moral rights, the book tells the stories of animal advocates' personal development (including Regan's) and discusses the influence of the media and animal use industries have in shaping how people often address ethics and animals. The best general introduction to ethics & animals issues.

3. Mark Rowlands, *Animals Like Us* (Verso, 2002).

   According to PETA (People for the Ethical Treatment of Animals) some people think *Animals Like Us* is the next *Animal Liberation*. Rowlands has other, more recent books on animals and ethics also, e.g., *Animal Rights: All That Matters* and others.

Good discussion and commentary are found in these books, which are recommend reading:

4. Lori Gruen, *Ethics and Animals: An Introduction* (Cambridge University Press, 2011): http://www.lorigruen.com/

   This book provides both original arguments, beyond those from the authors above, and insights and reviews and comments on many of the theories from Singer and Regan.

5. Angus Taylor, *Animals and Ethics: An Overview of the Philosophical Debate, 3rd edition* (Broadview 2009). A nice overview of the literature. (On Amazon.)

   This is a good "secondary source" that gives an overview of the many philosophical positions on theoretical and practical issues concerning ethics and animals.

LEARNING OUTCOMES

At the conclusion of this book, readers will be able to:

- understand basic, fundamental concepts, theories, and methods of reasoning from general ethics
- apply these ethical concepts to specific moral issues concerning animals;
- demonstrate stronger general skills in analyzing logic, critical thinking, and moral argument analysis;
- identify and evaluate arguments defending or opposing particular uses of animals, and theoretical claims about our obligations toward animals;
- understand the most influential moral arguments and positions given in defense of animals and for greater animal protection, these arguments' similarities and differences, the most common and influential objections that are raised against them, and how these arguments' advocates respond in defense of their positions;
- understand the most influential moral arguments and positions given in defense of animal use and against increased animal protection, these arguments' differences, the most common and influential objections that are raised against them and how these arguments' advocates might respond in defense of their positions;
- understand and be able to evaluate claims about the morally-relevant empirical information needed to make informed moral judgments on ethics and animals issues;
- understand what implications the various theories of ethics have for practical, concrete uses of animals, e.g., for food, for clothing, for experimentation, for entertainment, etc., as well as stronger skills at identifying and evaluating other reasons given for and against such uses of animals;
- more deeply develop their own views on the nature of our obligations to animals and be abler to provide moral defenses of their views and respond to critical objections and questions.

CONTENTS

CHAPTER 1: INTRODUCTION TO ETHICS, LOGIC AND ETHICS & ANIMALS

These chapters are intended to provide background to the readings, highlight important issues in the readings, introduce readings, and raise questions. This first chapter is longer than the rest.

Overview

Discussions of animal ethics are more fruitful when approached after an exposure to general thinking about ethics and methods of moral argument analysis. Theories of animal ethics are typically extensions or modifications of theories developed for addressing more familiar (and often less controversial) questions about human-to-human ethics. Therefore, it is important to be familiar with these theories and methods. These online readings will introduce readers to the more influential moral theories and methods of moral argument analysis, and we will read the introductions to our texts on animal ethics.

Readings

James Pryor (NYU Philosophy), Guidelines on Reading Philosophy:
http://www.jimpryor.net/teaching/guidelines/reading.html

Readings on argument analysis:

Since *arguments* for and against various uses of animals often have as a *premise* a *moral principle* derived from an *ethical theory*, we will first learn some basic concepts about arguments. We will then survey some ethical theories, some arguments in favor of some of them (i.e., reasons given to think that a theory is true), and some arguments against some of them (i.e., reasons given to think that a theory is false).

James Rachels, "Some Basic Points About Arguments," from

his *The Right Thing To Do: Basic Readings in Moral Philosophy*, 4*th* *Ed.* (McGraw Hill, 2007) (Google).

James Pryor, "What Is an Argument?"
http://www.jimpryor.net/teaching/vocab/argument.html

Readings that introduce common moral theories (and critique some of them):

- James Rachels, "A Short Introduction to Moral Philosophy," from *The Right Thing To Do* (Google)
- Tom Regan, "The Case for Animal Rights," from Tom Regan and Peter Singer, eds., *In Defense of Animals* (Blackwell, 1985): http://ethicsandanimals.googlepages.com/regancase_for_animal_rights.pdf ; also available here: http://www.animal-rights-library.com/texts-m/regan03.htm

Our texts' *short* prefaces and introductions:
ANIMAL LIBERATION – Preface to the 1975 Edition
ANIMAL LIBERATION – Preface to the 1990 Edition
ANIMAL LIBERATION – Preface to the 2002 Edition

EMPTY CAGES – FORWARD by Jeffrey Moussaieff Masson
EMPTY CAGES – PROLOGUE: The Cat
EMPTY CAGES – EPILOGUE: The Cat

EMPTY CAGES – PART I NORMAN ROCKWELL AMERICANS
EMPTY CAGES – 1. Who Are You Animal Rights Advocates Anyway?
EMPTY CAGES – 2. How Did You Get That Way?

Part I of *Empty Cages* discusses the influence the media and special interest politics have on how ethics & animals issues are typically approached. It also explains some different routes people might take to becoming involved in animal issues and Regan's tells the personal story of how he became an Animal Rights Advocate. This part of the book is, strictly speaking, not philosophy or ethics (but it surely relevant to ethics) and is an interesting, easy read.

ANIMALS LIKE US – Editor's Introduction
ANIMALS LIKE US – Introduction

Optional: Gruen, preface, and introductory matter.

Readers should sign up for these online email lists to keep up on major media coverage of issues concerning ethics and animals:

Dawnwatch News Service: http://dawnwatch.com
Vegan Outreach's E-Newsletter:
http://www.veganoutreach.org/enewsletter/index.html

Some of the links on the readings might be incorrect. Please Google the title and you will likely find the file online.

Moral Questions

In this book we will attempt to reasonably answer moral or ethical questions concerning the treatment and use of animals.[1] Some of these questions are general[2], e.g.:

- Morally, how should we treat animals?
- Which uses of animals, if any, are morally permissible, and which are morally wrong?
- Do we have any moral obligations toward any animals? What is the *extent* of these obligations? *Why* do we have these obligations (if we do)? What is it *about* (various kinds of) animals that *make* them such that how we treat them matters morally?
- Are there different obligations toward different animals? Might certain uses of some animals be morally permissible, whereas using other animals in similar ways would be wrong? (E.g., might some experiments be wrong if done on chimpanzees, whereas morally permissible, or perhaps "less wrong," if done on mice?
- Morally, should we be concerned only with certain kinds of animals, e.g., those who are conscious and have feelings? What about insects? What about unicellular organisms? On what basis do we decide?

---

[1] The terms 'ethical' and 'moral' will be used synonymously throughout this course.
[2] These questions might be described as being about the "moral status" of animals. I will not use this term however, since it is better to just ask straightforward questions about whether some treatment or use is morally permissible or not (and why), whether some treating some being (e.g., some animal) one way would be better or worse than treating another being (e.g., some human being) in a similar way, and so on.

Other questions deal with specific uses of animals, e.g.:

- Is it morally permissible to trap and skin animals for their fur in our society, where alternatives to fur coats are readily available? If we lived somewhere where there were no such "alternative" means to keep warm would that make a difference to the morality of using animals for their fur?
- Is it morally permissible to raise and kill animals to eat them in our society, where nutritious alternatives to animal foods are readily available? If we were somewhere where there were inadequate non-animal foods would that make a difference to the morality of using animals for food?
- If it could be known, with certainty, that some experiments on animals would save the lives of many human beings (or even just one?), would these experiments be morally permissible? If there was only a slight chance that these experiments would lead to such benefits, or no chance, would this make a difference to the morality of these experiments?

While everyone has answers to these questions, we are not interested in anyone's *mere* "opinions" or "feelings" about how they should be answered. We want to find out which answers are backed by the *best moral reasons* or *strongest moral arguments*, i.e., the arguments that we have the strongest reasons to believe are sound. We want to know *why* we should accept some answers to these questions and reject others. To do this we will attempt to improve out skills at reasoning morally.[1]

---

[1] We will challenge our own answers to questions like these above and arguments in favor of them by considering contrary answers to these questions (i.e., answers that contradict your, and perhaps *our*, answers). If we carefully identify evaluate the arguments given by people we disagree with, we may find that their arguments are stronger than our own and so we should change our minds! Another possibility is that their beliefs about how animals should be treated

What the Question Is Not: Not "Morally Right," but Morally Permissible and/or Morally Obligatory

One might think that the core questions in animal ethics are whether various uses of animals are *morally right* or *morally wrong*. This is not quite correct. Effective moral reasoning requires the clear and precise uses of words. Thus, when a word is ambiguous (i.e., has more than one meaning), we must identify these meanings and make it clear what meaning we are using. That way everyone knows what exact thought we have in mind when we make claims using that word: we're on the same page and can communicate effectively. And we can think about whether what we are saying is true or false and supported (or support*able*) by reasons and evidence or not.

This applies to the use of the word 'right,' as in *morally right* because the word is ambiguous. Examples show this. Suppose you saved a drowning baby by pulling her out of the bathtub. This was easy for you, not risky, and had you not been there the baby surely would have drowned. If someone says, "Your saving that baby was morally right," this person probably means to say that your saving that baby, in these circumstances, was *morally obligatory, morally required*, or a moral *duty*: if you had *not* saved the baby, you

---

should change and, perhaps, their behaviors toward animals should change also. Although change – in belief, attitude, feeling, action and policy – is a focus of this course, it is not about persuasion in the way that a course on advertising, marking, propaganda, and public / media relations might be. It is about persuasion, however, in that we are trying to identify which views people *should* persuaded to accept, if we wish to think critically and carefully about what we morally ought to do. *If* we are capable of such critical moral thinking (and, if so, *how* this is done) will be discussed below and in the readings on logic and argument analysis and practiced throughout the course.

would have done something *wrong* or *morally impermissible*.[1]

Consider another example. Although you are a person of average income, you send $1000 a month to famine relief organizations to help starving children. Someone says, "Your making these donations is morally right." Here this person probably does *not* mean to say your making these donations are *morally obligatory*, *morally required*, or a moral *duty*. Unlike the bathtub case, the common (but perhaps mistaken[2]) view is that your *not* donating would *not* be wrong or morally *im*permissible. So, this person probably means to by saying, at least, that what you do is *morally permissible*, i.e., *not wrong* or *not* morally *im*permissible. She might also mean that it is not merely permissible, but more positively good beyond that, but definitely not *morally obligatory*.

With these distinctions in mind, we can stop using an ambiguous word – "morally right" – and instead use these more precise terms categories for morally evaluating actions:

1. **morally permissible**: morally OK; *not* morally wrong; *not* morally *im*permissible; "OK to do";
2. **morally obligatory**: morally required; a moral duty; impermissible to not do it; wrong to not do it; "gotta do it";
3. **morally impermissible**: morally wrong; not permissible; obligatory to not do it; a duty to not do it.

We might also add a category "between" the permissible and the

---

[1] Of course, if story is that you didn't save the baby because you *can't* because you are paralyzed, or because you were already maxed-out saving 12 other drowning babies, then you weren't obligated to save *this* baby.

[2] Perhaps, however, "common sense" is mistaken and affluent people are morally obligated to make donations like these. For arguments for this conclusion, see (among other sources) Peter Singer's "Famine, Affluence and Morality" *Philosophy and Public Affairs*, vol. 1, no. 1 (Spring 1972), pp. 229-243 (Google) and his "The Singer Solution to World Poverty," *New York Times*, 1999 (Google).

obligatory for actions that are positively good, virtuous or admirable, and thereby morally permissible, but not obligatory: e.g., some argue that vegetarianism is in that category, and if this is correct then arguments for the conclusion that vegetarianism is morally obligatory are unsound. This category might be described as the "supererogatory," meaning beyond the call of duty or what's morally required.

Thus, the core questions in ethics and animals are what moral categories specific uses of animals fall into – morally permissible, morally obligatory, or morally impermissible or wrong – and, *most importantly*, *why*. Again, the *reasons* given for why we should think, e.g., that some use is permissible and another use is wrong, or whatever conclusions anyone advocates, are our main interest.

What the Questions Also Is Not: Not (Necessarily) Animal "Rights"

A second possible interpretation of the core questions of animal ethics is that they are about whether animals have "rights." On this view, to ask whether various uses of animals are morally permissible or not is *just to ask* whether animals have rights or not. It is very common for these two notions to be equated, but they shouldn't be, for a variety of reasons.

Legal Rights: Not the Issue

First, the term 'rights' is multiply ambiguous. One kind of rights are *legal* rights. Legal rights are such that, in theory, if they are violated, somebody can be punished by the criminal system. Legal rights are "man-made" and vary by time and location: the legal rights women have in the US differ from the legal rights women have in, e.g., Afghanistan. To figure out what legal rights animals have is often easy: just check the law books. There you would find that there are few laws that protect animals from harm: they have few legal rights.

Legal rights are not of much interest to us as ethicists, however, because what's legally permitted need not be morally permissible: e.g., slaveholding in the US South hundreds of years ago was legal yet immoral; and what's legally required may not be morally permissible: e.g., the legal requirement that drugs be "tested" on animals might be an immoral requirement. Although legal standards can be sometimes seen as a highly imperfect expression of a society's general views on what's moral and immoral, we will generally not discuss the law beyond our readings' occasionally observations that animals have few legal rights.

Moral Rights: Not *Necessarily* the Issue

A second possible kind of rights are *moral* rights. What are moral rights? Later Chapters will address some common misunderstandings and resulting confusions about moral rights, but the most important reason to not equate the questions of what uses of animals are permissible and whether animals have moral rights is this: although this might sound odd to some people, it's possible that many uses of animals are wrong *even though* animals have *no* moral rights. Various uses of animals might be wrong for *other* moral reasons besides their having rights, so *even if animals have no rights, it doesn't immediately follow that harmful animal use is morally permissible*. Equating the two issues conceals this possibility.

Again, the core questions in ethics and animals are what moral categories we should think specific uses of animals fall into – morally permissible, morally obligatory, or morally impermissible/wrong – and the reasons why we should think this. Thinking in terms of moral rights can make the issues more confusing than they have to be.

Some Basic Concepts about Arguments: Introduction to Logic

To attempt to try to figure out which moral views about animals are correct, we will try to find out which views are supported by the best reasons. To do this, will identify and evaluate *arguments*. The James Rachels ("Some Basic Points About Arguments" (Google) and James Pryor (at http://www.jimpryor.net/teaching/vocab/index.html) readings give excellent overviews of what arguments are and what makes arguments good and bad.

An **argument** is a conclusion that is supported by premises. The premises should lead to the conclusion, forming a "chain" of reasoning: this makes the argument "**logically valid**" (a technical term with a precise meaning that differs from how non-philosophers often might use the term). In a valid argument, since the premises lead to the conclusion (and this chain of reasoning is clearly identifiable), *if* the premises are true, *then* the conclusion must be true as well. When an argument is valid and the premises are true, then the argument is **sound** (and the conclusion is thereby true, given the definition of "valid" and the fact that the premises are true). If the argument is valid and, with good reasons, you think the premises are true, then you should think the argument is sound. We want to find sound arguments and reject unsound ones.

Our main concern is finding the arguments, understanding what exact conclusion(s) is being defended and what exact premises are given in its favor. We have to figure out whether the premises lead to the conclusion, i.e., is valid, or if we can "tweak" the argument by adding premises to make it valid. We then try to figure out if it is sound. Here are three rules for carefully identifying arguments:

1. Make the stated conclusion(s) and premise(s) *precise* in quantity: is something said to be true (or false) of *all* things (or people, or animals, etc.), or just *some* of them (and if so, which ones?)?
2. Clarify the intended meaning(s) of unclear or ambiguous words in conclusions or premises.
3. State (any) *assumed* premises so that the *complete* pattern of reasoning in an argument is displayed and it is clear how the stated premise(s) logically leads to the conclusion.

Other important logical tools are that of *necessary condition*(s), *sufficient condition*(s), *necessary and sufficient condition*(s), and *counterexamples*. (See Pryor especially). The importance of these concepts for animal ethics will be apparent as we work through the issues.

28

Moral Principles as Premises: Introduction to Ethics

Moral arguments often have a *moral principle* as a premise. We will attempt to figure out if these premises are true. Moral principles often assert that an action having some feature(s) is a *sufficient* condition(s) for that action being morally wrong, permissible, or whatever. E.g., here are two *possible* moral principles:

    A. *If* an action causes pain, *then* that action is morally wrong.
    B. *If* an action benefits someone and harms nobody, *then* that action is morally permissible.

(Can principle A can be refuted, i.e., shown false, by *counterexamples*, an exception to the proposed rule? Is principle B true? How would we try to figure that out?). Moral principles might also claim that an action having some feature(s) is a *necessary* condition for that action being morally wrong, permissible, or whatever, e.g.:

    C. A being has a "right to not suffer needlessly" *only if* that being is capable of reasoning morally.

(Can principle C be refuted, i.e., shown false, by counterexamples?).

Moral principles are often justified by appeal to *moral* or *ethical theories*. A moral theory attempts to answer these kinds of questions:

- What *makes* morally right actions right and wrong actions wrong? (Or, what *makes* permissible acts permissible, obligatory actions obligatory, etc.?)? What is it *about* actions that give them the moral status (permissible, obligatory, etc.) that they have?
- What's the basic, fundamental, essential difference(s) between permissible and impermissible actions? What features of actions mark that divide?

- What are the *necessary and sufficient conditions* for an action being permissible, obligatory, etc.?

Before looking at influential theories developed and refined by philosophers, it is useful to start by developing your own moral theory (or theories). Here is one method to do that:

Make a chart with three columns. In the left column, make a long list of actions (and we can use character traits too, if you'd like) that you think most people would think are *obviously wrong or bad*. In the right column, make a long list of actions or character traits that you think most people would think are *obviously morally permissible, obligatory or otherwise good*. In the middle, list any actions that come to mind but don't fall into either category. Share your list with others to compare, change, revise, etc.[1]

Now ask, what is it *about* the wrong actions on your list that *makes* them wrong? *Why* are they on the "wrong" list? What is it about the right/good actions that *make* them right or good? Why do they belong on that list? What moral hypotheses best explains this? Your answers here could result in your revising your initial judgments if you see that some emerging moral principles are inconsistent with any initial judgment.

A complementary approach is this:

Describe how animals are treated in, e.g., the food industry, the fur industry, in experimentation, etc. Would treating (any?) human beings in these ways be morally permissible, or would

---

[1] From Christina Hoff-Sommers' "Teaching The Virtues" (Google): "It is wrong to mistreat a child, to humiliate someone, to torment an animal. To think only of yourself, to steal, to lie, to break promises. Torturing a child. Starving someone to death. Humiliating an invalid in a nursing home. On the positive side: it is right to be considerate and respectful of others, to be charitable and generous."

this be wrong? What moral *hypotheses* – about what makes wrong actions wrong – *best explain* why this is so, e.g., why it would be wrong to treat humans in these ways?

These exercises might result in you developing basic theories that are similar to many influential moral theories that have been developed over the last few centuries, if not longer. Thinking for yourself can lead to many of the same moral insights many of the philosophical "greats" have had.

James Rachels, in "A Short Introduction to Moral Philosophy" (Google) and Tom Regan ("The Case for Animal Rights" *article*, not book; Google) discuss the (arguably) more plausible moral theories last after they discuss and sometimes argue against the (arguably) inferior theories. Here are the theories they discuss:

- **Relativism & Moral Skepticism** (Rachels, "Short Introduction" 2-3; Rachels "Basic Points About Arguments," 22-27)
  - o   Rachels argues relativism and skepticism are false.
- **Divine Command Theory** (Rachels "Short Introduction" 3-5)
  - o   Rachels argues the divine command theory is false and even that religious believers should not accept it. (See below on religion and ethics).
- **Virtue Theory** (Rachels, "Short Introduction" 5-6); "Cruelty-Kindness" (Regan, 217)
  - o   Regan argues that a kind of virtue theory, which he calls the cruelty-kindness view, is mistaken.
- **Natural Law** (Rachels, "Short Introduction" 6-8). Not a very popular theory any more outside of some Catholic contexts.
- **Contractarianism / the Social Contract** (Rachels "Short Introduction" 8-10); Regan (214-216). (Regan also discusses Rawls' improved version of contractarianism; Mark Rowlands modifies this theory to argue in defense of animals.)
  - o   Regan argues that contractarianisms are false.

- **Utilitarianism** (Rachels "Short Introduction" 11-14; Regan 217-220)
  - o Regan argues that utilitarianism is false.
- **Immanuel Kant's Ethics** ("Short Introduction" 17-19); **"The Rights View"** (Regan 220-223), which is developed out of a modification of Kant's 2nd Categorical Imperative; Regan has a broader view of who should be treated as "ends in themselves."

Here are two categories for ethical theories:

- ***Altruistic Ethical Theories*** (Rachels "Short Introduction" 10-11): a broad *category* of ethical theories; they contrast with "egoistic" theories where the only intrinsic moral concern is for yourself and how your actions affect your own interest.
- ***Ethical Theories that Require Impartiality*** (Rachels "Short Introduction" 14-16): a broad *category* of ethical theories; contrasts with "partialist" theories that allow special preference to family and friends.

Animal advocates typically argue that the moral theory(s) that best explain how we ought to treat human beings (especially vulnerable human beings: the very young and very old) have positive implications for animals. Whether their arguments are sound, we shall see.

Religion and Ethics: A Brief Comment

Ethical issues are sometimes addressed in the context of religion; indeed, it's often assumed that the two are inseparable. For this book, we will reject this assumption, largely for the reasons that Rachels presents, following Socrates. Their reasoning is this:

If some religious text, authority, or even God makes a moral judgment (e.g., about whether some use of animals is morally permissible or not, or any other moral topic), then either there

32

are *reasons* that justify that judgment or not. If there are no reasons supporting that judgment, then it is arbitrary and should not be accepted. If there *are* reasons, however, then those reasons are what justify the judgment, not the fact that some authority says so, and we should be able to identify and evaluate those reasons directly.

In sum, "Because I said so!" is not a good reason to believe something, unless whatever is said is supported by reasons. Nevertheless, there are many religiously-motivated animal advocacy organizations and thinkers and the suggested readings and web pages reference them.

Introduction to Animal Ethics

Finally, we will read the prefaces and introductions to our main texts. They are all interesting; Singer's is especially important to the historic development of the animal movement. We can use Regan's "cat case" and its variants as a unifying theme for inquiry. We will try to determine which broad view below is supported by the best moral reasons:

A. Any (or almost any) use of animals is morally permissible; there are no moral obligations to animals.
B. Seriously harming animals (e.g., causing them pain and suffering, killing them, etc.) is morally permissible provided they are housed in comfortable cages.
C. Seriously harming animals is permissible provided they are housed in comfortable cages, treated gently and killed painlessly.
D. Seriously harming animals is typically morally wrong, *even if* they are housed in comfortable cages, treated gently and killed painlessly.

Discussion Questions

1. For many ethical issues, a good place to start is to reflect

on "common views" about the issues. Suppose you surveyed a range of people about the moral questions that these Chapters open with. What are some of the most common answers that would be given? What *reasons* would you often hear in favor of these answers? Are these reasons generally good reasons or not? Why?

2. Based on the readings about logic and arguments, explain (i) what an argument is, (ii) what makes arguments good or bad (e.g., explain the concepts of validity and soundness), and (iii) what one does to try to show that an argument is sound or unsound (e.g., explain the concept of a counterexample). If you have any other questions about what arguments are and how to identify and evaluate them, ask them here. We will be practicing identifying and evaluating arguments throughout the course.

3. Complete the moral theory building exercises above. What does your moral theory (or theories) look like? According to your theory(s), what is it about wrong actions that seem to *make* them wrong, and what is it about morally permissible / obligatory / good actions that *make* them like that? What follows from your theory (or theories) for how human beings should be treated? What follows for animals (and *which* animals)?

4. Which moral theory (or theories) that Rachels and Regan discuss seem best, i.e., most likely to identify the (approximate) truth about the nature of morally permissible and obligatory actions? Which seems worst, i.e., false? Why?

5. What observations do you have about the Prefaces, Introductions, and Prologs to each of the books on animal ethics? What strikes you as interesting, provocative, controversial and otherwise worthy of comment and reflection?

Of course, always feel free to raise any other questions, observations, criticisms and any other responses to the Chapter's readings and issues.

CHAPTER 2: WHAT ARE (SOME) ANIMALS LIKE? ANIMAL MINDS AND HARMS TO ANIMALS

Overview

If any animals have minds, and thus are conscious, then they can be harmed, and thus how they are treated raises moral issues. And, arguably, there are moral obligations towards animals *only if* they have minds, so questions about animal ethics very much depend on what animals are like. This Chapter we will get an overview of the scientific and philosophical literature on whether any animals are conscious, whether any are sentient (i.e., capable of sensation or feeling, especially of pleasures and pains), and so whether various species of animals have minds and, if so, what their mental, psychological and/or emotional lives might be like. We will discuss how anyone could know or reasonably believe some claim about animals' minds.

Readings

Note: some of the discussion of animal minds immediately overlaps with ethical questions, but we will attempt to focus this week just on animal minds.

ANIMALS LIKE US – Ch. 1. Do Animals Have Minds? pp. 3 – 25.
ANIMALS LIKE US – Ch. 4. Killing Animals. pp. 70 – 99.

ANIMAL LIBERATION – pp. 9 – 22, beginning "There is, however, one general defense of the practices...", ending on the first paragraph on 22.

EMPTY CAGES – pp. 53 – 61.

Gruen: 1. Why animals matter (optional)

Recommended Reading on Animal Minds / Cognitive Ethology:

- Colin Allen (http://mypage.iu.edu/~colallen/), "Animal Consciousness," entry in Stanford Encyclopedia of Philosophy: http://plato.stanford.edu/entries/consciousness-animal/
- Jonathan Balcombe, *Pleasurable Kingdom: Animals and The Nature of Feeling Good* (MacMillan 2006) http://www.pleasurablekingdom.com/
- Marc Bekoff's web page and books: http://literati.net/Bekoff/
- Clare Palmer, "Animals in Anglo-American Philosophy" http://www.h-net.org/~animal/ruminations_palmer.html
- Scott Wilson, "Animals and Ethics," *The Internet Encyclopedia of Philosophy* http://www.iep.utm.edu/a/anim-eth.htm
- Lori Gruen, "The Moral Status of Animals," *The Stanford Encyclopedia of Philosophy*, http://plato.stanford.edu/entries/moral-animal/

Being Specific About Species

In the first Chapter on logic, I made these two suggestions about identifying arguments:

- Make the stated conclusion(s) and premise(s) *precise* in quantity: is something said to be true (or false) of *all* things (or people, or animals, etc.), or just *some* of them (and if so, which ones?)?
- Clarify the intended meaning(s) of unclear or ambiguous words in conclusions or premises.

These suggestions are relevant to thinking about animals' minds since the category of "animal" is extremely broad: "animals" range from unicellular organisms, insects, invertebrates, vertebrates, birds, and to mammals of different kinds, including primates (like human beings). Since there are millions of species of animals, so when investigating whether animals' have minds, the natural questions are, "*Which* animals?" or, "What do you *mean* by 'animals'? Which animals are you referring to?"

Sometimes we forget to notice that these same questions should often be asked about human beings' mental lives. The mental lives of, e.g., newborn babies, five-year-olds, "normal" adults, cognitively disabled individuals, and Alzheimer's patients surely differ greatly. So if someone says that (all) animals don't have minds like human beings' minds, we should ask *which* human beings, since many some, if not, many animals have mental lives comparable to, if not richer than, many human beings' minds. That's a possibility: whether we should think it's true, of course, depends on what the research shows about the varieties of animals' and humans' minds and mental capacities.

Our readings primarily focus on mammals and birds, although there is some discussion of fish, invertebrates (such as octopi) and even some research on insects. But, again, it seems likely the minds of different mammals (if any have minds) are also different: e.g., a mouse's mental life is likely quite different from a chimpanzee's (especially if that chimp has been taught sign language). Additional research on different kinds of animals' minds will be discussed in later sections of the course: e.g., research on the minds of chickens, cows, and pigs will be discussed in the sections on animal agriculture; rats and mice, cats, dogs and primates in the sections of animal experimentation, and so on.

How Do We Know? Arguments from Analogy & Inference to the Best Scientific Explanation

Epistemology is an area of philosophy that asks how we *know* things and what it is for a belief to be *reasonable* and supported by good *evidence*. How might we *know* that any animals have minds, or reasonably believe any such claims? We can call this question "The Epistemological Problem of Animal Minds."

Before we think about this (hard) problem, it's worthwhile to mention that philosophers (and some psychologists and neuroscientists) worry about a more general (hard) problem called "The Epistemological Problem of Other Minds" regarding *humans' minds*. The problem is that each of us only has "direct access" to our own perceptions, thoughts, and feelings: we cannot directly "see" that anyone else is conscious and has a mind. All we see is external, overt behavior (including speech) and, presumably, somehow *infer* from this behavior that another individual has thoughts, feelings, and perceptions somewhat like our own. Perhaps this inference is not consciously made, but how else could we know that other *people* have minds?!

Believe it or not, this question has troubled philosophers for millennia and there is no widely accepted answer. Many philosophers argue, however, that we know that other people have minds either by **reasoning by analogy** or by **reasoning from the best explanation of some phenomena**, in this case, the overt behavior.

To reason by analogy is, most simply, to reason like this:

- Thing 1 has these characteristics *a*, *b*, and *c*;
- Thing 2 has characteristics a & b;
- Thing 2 is *relevantly similar* to Thing 1;
- *Therefore*, *probably* Thing 2 has characteristic *c* too.

Or, even more simply: "These two things are similar in the relevant ways, so therefore what is true of one is probably true of the other." The strength of an argument from analogy depends on how similar to two things are: the more similar, the stronger the analogy, obviously, and more likely the conclusion is to be true. To respond to the "Problem of other Minds," someone might reason, "I behave these ways, have this kind of biology, and *I have a mind.* Other people behave in similar ways and have similar biology. *Therefore*, they probably have minds too." It's important to observe that we apparently often use the same kind of kind of reasoning about animals' minds, as our authors demonstrate.

The second common pattern of reasoning about minds is an argument from the best explanation:

- There is some event that requires explanation.
- Explanation or hypothesis E *best explains* that event (i.e., is a better explanation than other candidate explanations in that it makes sense of more of the data/observations, allows predication, is simpler, fits with pre-existing knowledge, etc.)
- *Therefore*, *probably* E, and what's entailed by E, are true.

This pattern of reasoning is often applied to animal behavior: an animal does something (e.g., reacts in some interesting way to new surroundings); we try to figure out if this reaction would be better explained on the hypothesis that (a) this animal is a mindless automaton or (b) this animal has a conscious mind (or some other explanation, perhaps with greater details than [b]). How this reasoning will work out *very much* depends on the details of the case, but it's important to note that we use this pattern of reasoning to investigate both humans' and animals' minds.

A Source of Doubts: Necessary Conditions for Having a Mind

Many who argue (or have argued, in the case of historical figures) that animals don't have minds often claim that there is (or are) *necessary condition(s)* for having a mind, animals lack that necessary condition, and therefore they are mindless. So, some have claimed that a being has a mind *only if*, e.g., that being has language, and argued that animals are mindless since they can't speak. Critics tend to challenge these claims by either arguing that that (some) animals meet this necessary condition or by arguing that it's false that this condition is a necessary one: a being can have a mind even if it lacks this condition. They also tend to point out that many such principles imply that human infants are mindless, which seems to be false (and perhaps *must* be false, since such infants do learn language, and that can happen only if they have minds already, before having language).

These are a few central concepts to keep in mind while reading the interesting and informative readings for this Chapter.

Discussion Questions

1. For many philosophical issues, a good place to start is to reflect on "common views" about the issues. Suppose you surveyed a range of people and asked them what the minds or mental lives of various species of animals are like, whether (any) animals are *conscious*, can *feel*, can *think*, can *reason*, have *emotions* and so on. What are some of the most common answers that would be given? What *reasons* would you often hear in favor of these answers? Are these reasons generally good reasons or not? Why?
2. There are historical and contemporary doubts that any animals possess minds. Summarize these doubts. Explain whether these doubts are reasonable or not, in your view.
3. What are animals' minds like, according to most contemporary scientists and philosophers? What kind of

mental states do (any) animals have, e.g., beliefs, desires, memory, reasoning, planning, expectations for the future, self-awareness, emotions, etc.? Summarize the research, focusing on different mental states for different species or kinds of animals, if appropriate.

4. How would one *know* or *reasonably believe* some claim about the mental states of animals? Explain what kind of reasoning processes and evidence philosophers, scientists and "ordinary people" appeal to when they argue that animals have minds.

5. What is it to "harm" someone? Can (any) animals be harmed? If so, which kinds of animals? How can they be harmed? Explain and defend your answers.

Of course, always feel free to raise any other questions, observations, criticisms and any other responses to the Chapter's readings and issues.

Paper option

First, please read Jim Pryor's "Guidelines on Writing a Philosophy Paper" at http://www.jimpryor.net/teaching/guidelines/writing.html

Assignment

For an audience unfamiliar with any of the material of this course, write a short paper where you present and discuss the most important arguments for the view that *some animals have minds*. Be specific about what kinds of animals you are discussing, what you mean by "minds," and explain the variety of reasons why someone should believe that these animals have minds. Although this might seem like "common sense," people have doubted that animals have minds; therefore, explain the best or most common objections to the view that animals have minds, i.e., arguments that animals do not have minds. Explain what you think people should think about this issue and why.

CHAPTER 3: IN DEFENSE OF ANIMALS: SOME MORAL ARGUMENTS

Overview

This chapter will survey the most influential "theories of animal ethics," i.e., general theories that attempt to explain the nature and extent of our moral obligations toward animals, which have been used to argue in defense of animals. As we will see, these theories are often extensions or developments of the moral theories that have been developed to explain how humans ought to treat other human beings. These thinkers often argue that the moral theory (or theories) that *best explain* the nature and extent of our moral obligations to human beings (especially vulnerable ones, such as babies, children, the mentally challenged, the elderly, and so on) have positive implications for many animals as well. Thus, they often argue that there are no *relevant differences* between the kinds of cases to justify protecting human beings but allowing serious harms to animals and, therefore, animals are due moral protections comparable to at least those given to comparably-conscious, aware, sentient human beings.

Readings

ANIMAL LIBERATION – 1. All Animals Are Equal . . . or why the ethical principle on which human equality rests requires us to extend equal consideration to animals too

EMPTY CAGES – PART II MORAL RIGHTS: WHAT THEY ARE AND WHY THEY MATTER
EMPTY CAGES – 3. Human Rights
EMPTY CAGES – 4. Animal Rights (entire chapter or until p. 62, where objections begin: this section will be re-assigned below)

Videos: Tom Regan:
From 2006, "Animal Rights: An Introduction": (at
https://www.youtube.com/watch?v=fTNNJspZXA4)

44

From 1989, "Does the animal kingdom need a bill of rights?"[1] (at https://www.youtube.com/watch?v=xj-MJKFM0Zs)

ANIMALS LIKE US – Ch. 2. The Moral Club

Gruen: 2. The natural and the normative (optional)

---

[1] "To the best of my recollection, the speech I gave, as presented on YouTube, was given in 1989, in London, under the auspices of the Royal Institution of Great Britain. It was part of a debate over the question, 'Does the animal kingdom need a bill of rights?' I spoke in favor of the proposal, as did Andrew Linzey and Richard Ryder. Germaine Greer and Mary Warnock spoke against it. For its time, the event was a big deal. As I recall, the BBC televised it throughout the UK on one of the national channels. The room (it was a formal setting, in a regal hall) was packed, those in the audience as respectful as they were attentive. I do not think there was any formal, or informal, vote on the question. So who won the debate is not something anyone can know. I do know, though, that it was a memorable event in my life. For me, personally, I had never before (and have not since) had the opportunity to address so many people, at one time, and in so many different places, on the philosophy of animal rights. I will never forget it." – Tom Regan, 2007

General Theories and Particular Cases

This Chapter will get an initial presentation of three of the most influential methods of moral thinking for *human to human* interactions that have been extended to apply to *human to animal* interactions, i.e., how humans ought to treat non-human animals. These perspectives are, first, a demand for equality or *equal moral consideration of interests* (developed by Peter Singer; however he sometimes describes his ethical theory as a form of *utilitarianism,* although his book *Animal Liberation* does not presuppose it); second, a demand for respect of *the moral right to respectful treatment* (developed by Tom Regan); and, third, a demand that moral decisions be made *fairly and impartially* and the use of a novel thought experiment designed to ensure this (developed by Mark Rowlands, following John Rawls, the most influential political philosopher of the twentieth century).

We want to *try* to focus on these theories in themselves and their implications for animals "in general," without so much focus on what they imply for particular uses of animals, e.g., for food, fashion experimentation, entertainment, and other purposes. This attempt to make things a bit more abstract and general might seem forced, and we will surely understand the theories more deeply more when we see them applied to particular cases. Nevertheless, we want to try to evaluate these theories as true or false, well-supported or not, on their own terms.

Arguments from Paradigm Cases: Inference to the Best Moral Explanation

Earlier we saw that scientists (and philosophers) sometimes use a pattern of reasoning known as *inference to the best explanation* to explain non-moral phenomena, e.g., the existence of minds. Ethicists use this form of reasoning also, although what is usually being explained is some clear moral intuition, or a moral judgment that nearly everyone agrees on (and seemingly for good reason). Again, the pattern is something like this:

- A moral judgment – J – seems true, and what *makes* it true requires explanation.
- Moral explanation or hypothesis T *best explains* the truth of J (i.e., T is a better explanation than other candidate explanations in that it makes sense of more of the data/observations/similar moral intuitions, allows us to make other moral judgments (thus enabling a kind of prediction, perhaps), is simpler, fits with pre-existing knowledge, etc.)
- *Therefore, probably* T, and what's entailed by T, are true.

Singer seems to use this pattern of reasoning, starting with the widely accepted moral judgments that *racism and sexism (and other prejudices) are wrong*. He gives an analysis of what racism and sexism *are* – they are not easy to define – and gives an explanation for *why* they are wrong, arguing that this explanation is a better explanation than some rival explanations. He then argues that this explanation, which appeals to *the principle of equality of consideration of interests,* has positive implications for animals. Since many animals have interests, the prejudice that results in their interests being ignored is *speciesism.*

Regan argues similarly, starting with the informed intuition that the men in the Tuskegee Syphilis Study were treated wrongly (p. 44; elsewhere he uses historical cases of harmful medical experiments on retarded children[1]). He argues that the *best explanation* why they way these men (and children) were treated was wrong has positive implications for animals. He argues that these men had moral rights to life, bodily integrity, and respectful treatment. He develops the "subject of a life" sufficient condition for having basic moral rights to life, to bodily integrity and respectful treatment, shows that this criterion for moral rights applies to many animals as well, and that they thereby have moral rights as well.

---

[1] "Empty Cages: Animal Rights & Vivisection," essay at
http://tomreganemptycages.blogspot.com/

In both cases, the pattern is to start with what we are confident with, think about the best reasons to support that confident judgment, and see that that these reasons have implications for areas that we perhaps have not thought about as carefully. We then see that that we have to revise our previous judgments about that new kind of case or, *if we are to be consistent,* revise our initial judgments (e.g., about the human cases), or argue that nothing follows from one kind of case to another because they are relevantly dissimilar. Singer, Regan and Rowlands, as well as the others, are clear on the logical options.

Sufficient Conditions for Taking Someone's Interests Seriously

The cases for animals can be seen as an attempt to identify this '**this**' here:

> *If* a being is like *this* _____, *then* we must take its interests seriously, it's wrong to harm it (except for very good reasons), we must respect it, etc.

Animal advocates typically argue that if we look at what we think about human beings, it appears that we think (or should think) that *all* human beings, especially those who are vulnerable – the very young and old – deserve such protections: e.g., none should be eaten, worn and experimented on. These philosophers argue that, for human beings, we seem to think the 'this' above is just consciousness or sentience or, as Regan puts it, being a "subject of a life," and that this is a *sufficient condition* for it being the case that a being is wrong to harm. They argue that this principle applies to (some) animals as well, those animals that possess the relevant characteristics that humans have.

Most critics of this reasoning attempt to find other characteristics that would account for the wrongness of harming human beings, but seek characteristics that only human beings have and no animals have. The challenge is, first, finding these characteristics and, second, explaining why they are morally relevant.

Again, the Issue is Not (Necessarily) Animal "Rights"

To revisit an issue introduced in the first Chapter, sometimes people describe all "pro-animal" thinkers as "animal rights" advocates. This isn't correct: e.g., Singer, for one, argues in defense of animals without much mentioning any idea of rights. So, again, one can think that animals' interests must be taken seriously, that it's seriously wrong to harm animals in most circumstances, that animals have a high "moral status," etc., but not think that they have rights or, at least, not find that to be a useful way of presenting one's views.

But what are moral rights anyway? First, views that maintain that animals (and human beings) have moral rights are often moral theories that appeal to the idea of a moral right in explaining what *makes* wrong actions wrong and permissible actions permissible: usually they claim that an action is impermissible if it violates a right; thus, rights are constraints on behavior. We will examine two rights theories – Regan's and Rowlands' – in detail. While these theories typically support the view that most harmful uses of animals are morally permissible, the theory and the particular judgments about what's morally permissible are, strictly, speaking, distinct.

A bit about moral rights: moral rights, *if they exist*, are *not* "man made," and individuals who have right have them *even if* others do not recognize or acknowledge that. Moral rights are not "granted" or "given" by anyone: e.g., slaves had moral rights (to life, to liberty) *even though many people did not respect or acknowledge these rights*. When these moral rights were acknowledged or recognized, it is not the case that slaves were "given" or "granted" moral rights, since they already had them. Thus, sometimes people often ask whether animals should be "given" rights. Since *moral* rights are not "given," this question is founded on a mistaken assumption.

Moral rights are always a right *to* something or a right *from* something, e.g., a right *to* life or a right *from* interference. There are no generic moral rights – just plain moral rights – so if someone claims that animals have (or lack) moral rights, the question we must ask is, "A right *to what*, or right *from what?*" Here there are many candidates: rights to life, to respectful treatment, to not being caused to suffer, to not be harmed, to have their interests taken into consideration, to liberty, to not being considered "property," to not be "used" to benefit others, and on and on: there are many possible moral rights to consider.

Whenever we discuss a claim that animals have or lack moral rights, we need to be specific on which moral right(s) is under consideration. Some advocates of animal use have claimed that, e.g., animals have a *right* to be eaten, and a *right* to be skinned (alive!) for their fur, and thus calling themselves advocates of animal rights! Focusing on specific moral rights, such as rights to not be caused various kinds of harm, will prevent those who harm animals from being considered legitimate animal rights advocates.

Finally, appeals to moral rights can sometimes be "question begging," which means to say that they just assume the conclusion that's being defended, stating it in other words instead of supporting it. This can happen with other moral issues: someone might claim that abortion, i.e., killing unborn fetuses, is wrong because *unborn fetuses have a moral right to life.* Unless this person explains *why* fetuses have such a right, this argument *might* amount to just saying that killing fetuses is wrong *because* killing fetuses is wrong, which is just restating the conclusion as one's premise. Similarly, someone might say that eating animals is not wrong because humans have a moral right to eat them. Again, unless this person explains why we should think that we have this right, what might be said here is just that *eating animals is not wrong because it is not wrong for us to eat animals.* Since arguments should never just assume their conclusion, or merely restate it in different words, these arguments are no good.

Again, the core questions in ethics and animals are what moral categories we should think specific uses of animals fall into – morally permissible, morally obligatory, or morally impermissible/wrong – and the reasons why we should think this. Thinking in terms of moral rights can make the issues more confusing than they have to be.

50

Discussion Questions

1. For many ethical issues, a good place to start is to reflect on "common views" about the issues. Suppose you surveyed a range of people and asked them what kind of moral obligations we have towards animals (perhaps you should ask about specific animals or different kinds of animals). *Focusing on possible broadly "pro-animal" responses,* what are some of the most common answers that would be given? What *reasons* would you often hear in favor of these answers? Are these reasons generally good reasons or not? Why?

2. *For an audience who has not read the texts,* explain Singer's view about what moral obligations we have towards animals and his main arguments favor of that view. What questions and objections do you have for him? How would he respond? Are his arguments sound? Why or why not?

3. *For an audience who has not read the texts,* explain Regan's view about what moral obligations we have towards animals and his main arguments favor of that view. What questions and objections do you have for him? How would he respond? Are his arguments sound? Why or why not?

4. *For an audience who has not read the texts,* explain Rowlands' view about what moral obligations we have towards animals and his main arguments favor of that view. What questions and objections do you have for him? How would he respond? Are his arguments sound? Why or why not?

5. *Should* people find any (or all) of the cases given in defense of animals to be persuasive? Which, if any, is strongest, in your opinion, and why? If you think people should be persuaded, why is it that they often are not? (If people should *not* be persuaded, why are some people convinced?). Any other questions or objections from anything from this section can be asked here.

Of course, always feel free to raise any other questions, observations, criticisms and any other responses to the Chapter's readings and issues.

Paper Option

For an audience unfamiliar with ethics, logic and animal ethics, explain the strongest broad moral case to be made in defense of animals (this could be a single theorist's approach, or perhaps it could be a combination approach). Explain what this case implies in general for animals and how one defends or supports such a theory about how animals deserve to be treated. Raise and respond to at least three of what you think are the most important objections to your arguments or your position. 4-6 pages.

CHAPTER 4: OBJECTIONS TO DEFENSES OF ANIMALS AND DEFENDING ANIMAL USE

Overview

This Chapter we will survey the most influential general moral theories that have been appealed to argue in defense of animal use and/or to object to the theories developed in defense of animals. As we will see, these theories are often extensions or developments of the moral theories that have been developed to explain how humans ought to treat other human beings. These writers often argue that the moral theory (or theories) that *best explain* the nature and extent of our moral obligations to human beings (especially vulnerable ones, such as babies, children, the mentally challenged, the elderly, and so on) *do not* have positive implications for animals. Thus, they argue that there are *relevant differences* between the kinds of cases that justify protecting all human beings but allowing serious harms to animals.

Readings

EMPTY CAGES – 4. Animal Rights (pp. 62-74)

ANIMAL LIBERATION – 5. Man's Dominion . . . *a short history of speciesism* (See especially the discussion of Aquinas, Descartes, Kant and thinkers discussed in *The Enlightenment and After*)

Tibor Machan, "Why Animal Rights Don't Exist" at http://www.strike-the-root.com/4/machan/machan43.html and "The Myth of Animal Rights" at http://www.lewrockwell.com/machan/machan52.html Video: https://www.youtube.com/watch?v=s1HOtggYuMQ

Carl Cohen, "Why Animals Do Not Have Rights," from Cohen and Regan, *The Animal Rights Debate* (Rowman & Littlefield, 2001) at http://ethicsandanimals.googlepages.com/cohen-ardebate.pdf

Video: Carl Cohen, "Why Animals Do Not Have Rights": at
https://www.youtube.com/watch?v=kbk7xY9t-UQ

Ray Frey, "Animal Research: The Starting Point" (1-page
selection), from *Why Animal Experimentation Matters.*
http://ethicsandanimals.googlepages.com/frey-
experimentation.pdf (this file needs to be corrected)

ANIMAL LIBERATION – 1. All Animals Are Equal – review
the objections that Singer discusses

ANIMALS LIKE US – Ch. 2. The Moral Club – review the
objections that Rowlands discusses

General Theories and Particular Cases

Like the last Chapter, we want to *try* to focus on these theories in themselves and their implications for animals "in general," without so much focus on what they imply for particular uses of animals, e.g., for food, fashion experimentation, entertainment, and other purposes. This will likely be harder than the last Chapter because many objections to pro-animal theories come from particular cases, e.g. arguments like these:

1. Animal experimentation is morally permissible, if not obligatory.
2. But if Regan's theory is true, then animal experimentation is wrong.
3. Therefore, Regan's theory of animal rights is not true.

And:

1. There's nothing wrong with raising animals to eat them.
2. But if there's nothing wrong with raising animals to eat them, then animals' interests don't deserve equal consideration.
3. If animals' interests don't deserve equal consideration, then Singer's theory is false.
4. Therefore, Singer's theory is false.

Of course, we want to know for what *reasons* we should accept these first premises, especially if we are familiar with ethics! But perhaps a way to avoid some of these particular cases about animals at this time is to focus on what the theories of the critics of pro-animal thinking imply for human beings, especially the young, old, weak and powerless. Various kinds of contractarianisms support poor treatment of animals, but they seem to support poor treatment of humans as well, and so contractarians often feel a need to defend themselves from these objections. Maybe these theories can sometimes be better evaluated from the more neutral concern of human-to-human ethics.

In evaluating moral theories and thinking about ethics in general, you want to try to have your principles or theories have the right implications for particular cases and have those implications for the right reasons. Unfortunately, there is no exact formula for doing this! Ethics can be hard.

Necessary Conditions for Taking Someone's Interests Seriously: Cases Against Animals

While animal advocates focus on *sufficient conditions* for someone being in "The Moral Club" (as Rowlands puts it), anti-animal theorists tend to focus on *necessary conditions*, claiming that:

> We must take a being's interests seriously, it's wrong to harm it (except for very good reasons), we must respect it, etc., *only if* it is like this: ____.

They then typically fill in that blank with rather cognitively advanced abilities: sophisticated reasoning, thinking about one's thinking, intellectual achievement, religious worship, and so on. Their challenge, of course, comes from the fact that many human beings lack such sophisticated minds, yet we think we must take their interests seriously. This problem for anti-animal theorists is known as the "argument from marginal cases." To get around it, these theorists often attempt to do some intellectual acrobatics, trying to relate non-mentally sophisticated human beings (who seem to lack the stated necessary condition for, e.g., having any moral rights) to sophisticated human beings in peculiar ways. We will attempt to pin down their reasoning and see if it seems to be generally valid or is developed as an ad hoc response to this problem or worse.

Finding Relevant Differences from Arguments from Paradigm Cases: Inference to *Better* Moral Explanations?

Regarding above, anti-animal thinkers need to offer explanations of the clear cut cases of wrongs to human beings and *not* have those explanations have positive implications for animals.

Common Invalid Arguments

An argument is invalid when the premises do not logically lead to the conclusion. Many objections to cases against animals are of a common invalid argument form called "denying the antecedent," where the premises do not lead to the conclusion or the conclusion logically follow from the premises. This argument is invalid:

1. *If* conscious, sentient animals have moral rights *then* seriously harming them is typically wrong.
2. *But* animals *do not* have *any* moral rights.
3. *Therefore*, animal experimentation is morally *permissible*.

This argument is of the same invalid pattern as this argument:

1. If you (the reader) were a professional basketball player, then you would be over a foot tall. [TRUE!]
2. But you are *not* a professional basketball player. [TRUE!?]
3. *Therefore*, you are not over a foot tall. [FALSE]

Non-professional basketball players should see that these premises are true but the conclusion false: this means that the premises do not lead to the conclusion. The same is true about the first argument above since the pattern is the same. The point applies to this invalid argument too:

1. If animals are "equal" to humans, as "important" has humans, have the same "moral status" as humans, then seriously harming them is typically wrong.
2. But animals are not "equal" to humans, not as "important" has humans, and do have the same "moral status" as humans.
3. Therefore, seriously harming them is *not* typically wrong.

Furthermore, what it *means* to say these things about "equality," "importance," and "moral status" are not *at all* clear: much explanation would be needed for the kind of understanding needed to decide whether this claim is true or false.

Making the Discussion Concrete

Again, the core questions in ethics and animals are what moral categories we should think specific uses of animals fall into – morally permissible, morally obligatory, or morally impermissible / wrong – and the reasons why we should think this. This Chapter we should be trying to find the strongest, most important or at least most common and influential theories that would *seem* to support the conclusion that most (or any) routine, harmful uses of animals are just not morally wrong.

Discussion Questions

1. For many ethical issues, a good place to start is to reflect on "common views" about the issues. Suppose you surveyed a range of people and asked them what kind of moral obligations we have towards animals (perhaps you should ask about specific animals or different kinds of animals). *Focusing on possible broadly "anti-animal" responses (which some might describe as "pro-human"),* what are some of the most common answers that would be given? What *reasons* would you often hear in favor of these answers? Are these reasons generally good reasons or not? Why?

2. What are the strongest, most important and/or most interesting objections that critics raise to the moral cases in defense of animals? Are these objections successful, i.e., do they defeat any of the defenses of animals (from the last Chapter)? Are these arguments sound? Why or why not?

3. *For an audience who has not read the texts,* explain Kant's, Cohen's, and Machan's arguments against animals. What questions and objections do you have to them? How might they respond? Are their arguments sound? Why or why not?

4. *For an audience who has not read the texts,* explain the arguments "against animals" from contractarianism or the social contract theory (especially see Taylor's discussion of

Carruthers, and Regan's discussion of Narveson from Chapter 1). What questions and objections do you have for them? How might they respond? Are their arguments sound? Why or why not?

5. *Should* people find any (or all) of the cases "against animals" to be persuasive? Which, if any, is strongest, in your opinion, and why? If you think people should be persuaded, why is it that they often are not? (If people should *not* be persuaded, why are some people convinced?). Any other questions or objections from anything from this section can be asked here.

Of course, always feel free to raise any other questions, observations, criticisms and any other responses to the Chapter's readings and issues.

Paper option

Assignment: For an audience unfamiliar with ethics, logic and animal ethics, explain the strongest broad moral case to be made "against" animals and/or as a critical response to pro-animal ethical theorizing (this could be a single theorist's approach, or perhaps it could be a combination approach). Explain what this case implies in general for animals and how one defends or supports such a theory about how animals deserve to be treated. Raise and respond to at least three of what you think are the most important objections to your arguments or your position. 4-6 pages.

CHAPTER 5: WEARING AND EATING ANIMALS

Overview

Animal advocacy organization Vegan Outreach observes that "The number of animals killed for fur in the U.S. each year is approximately equal to the human population of Illinois. The number of animals killed in experimentation in the U.S. each year is approximately equal to the human population of Texas. The number of mammals and birds farmed and slaughtered in the U.S. each year is approximately equal *to one and two-thirds the entire human population of Earth*. Over 99% of the animals killed in the U.S. each year die to be eaten."[1] This Chapter we will focus on the moral arguments for and against using animals for fur and for food (as well as for different kinds of animal-food production, e.g., "factory farm" versus "traditional animal husbandry"), as well as the relationships between these arguments: what one thinks about the morality of the fur industry *might* have implications for the morality of meat, dairy and egg industries.

Readings

On the Fur Industry:

EMPTY CAGES – PART III SAYING AND DOING
EMPTY CAGES – 5. What We Learn from Alice
EMPTY CAGES – PART IV THE METAMORPHOSES
EMPTY CAGES – 7. Turning Animals into Clothes

OPTIONAL Reading & Viewing on the Fur Industry:
Fur industry representatives:
- Fur Commission USA, a non-profit association representing over 600 mink farmers in the United States http://www.furcommission.com See especially

---

[1] Matt Ball, "Activism and Veganism," at
http://www.veganoutreach.org/advocacy/path.html

the pages "Animal Rights versus Animal Welfare" and "Fur on Film"

- Fur Information Council of America: www.fur.org/
- National Animal Interest Alliance (defends *all* uses of animals, so relevant to all issues below also): http://www.naiaonline.org/about/index.htm

Critics of the fur industry:

- HSUS: http://www.hsus.org/furfree/,
- Mercy for Animals: http://www.mercyforanimals.org/fur_farms.asp,
- PETA: http://www.furisdead.com/,
- Tribe of Heart, producers of "The Witness" film: http://www.tribeofheart.org/

On the Animal Agriculture Industries:

EMPTY CAGES – 6. Turning Animals into Food

ANIMAL LIBERATION – 3. Down on the Factory Farm . . . or what happened to your dinner when it was still an animal
ANIMAL LIBERATION – 4. Becoming a Vegetarian . . . or how to produce less suffering and more food at a reduced cost to the environment

ANIMALS LIKE US – Ch. 5. Using Animals for Food

Gruen: 3. Eating animals (optional)

Jan Narveson, "A Defense of Meat Eating" (2 pages): http://ethicsandanimals.googlepages.com/narveson.pdf (See Rachels and Regan's discussions of contractarianism or the social contract from week one).

Temple Grandin, "Thinking Like Animals" (3 pages; last ½ page is where the "ethics" is offered): http://ethicsandanimals.googlepages.com/grandin.pdf

Ray Frey, "Utilitarianism and Vegetarianism Again: Protest or Effectiveness?":
http://ethicsandanimals.googlepages.com/frey-veg.pdf

Optional: Peter Singer & Jim Mason, Ch. 17, "The Ethics of Eating Meat," pp. 241- 273, from *The Way We Eat: Why Our Food Choices Matter* (Rodale 2006):
http://ethicsandanimals.googlepages.com/way-we-eat.pdf

Optional: The following sources, among others, are discussed in this chapter: Hugh Fearnley-Whittingstall's *The River Cottage Meat Book*: http://www.rivercottage.net/ (Amazon); Michael Pollan's "An Animals Place"
http://www.michaelpollan.com/article.php?id=55 and *The Omnivore's Dilemma*
http://www.michaelpollan.com/omnivore.php ; Roger Scruton's *Animal Rights and Wrongs* http://www.roger-scruton.com/rs-books.html ; Gaverick Matheny, "Least Harm: A Defense of Vegetarianism,"
http://www.jgmatheny.org/matheny%202003.pdf

Recommended Reading & Viewing:
Some advocates of animal agriculture:
National Institute of Animal Agriculture:
http://www.animalagriculture.org
American Meat Institute: http://www.meatami.com/
Animal Agriculture Alliance: http://www.animalagalliance.org
"Best Food Nation," http://www.bestfoodnation.com/

National Chicken Council:
http://www.nationalchickencouncil.com/
US Poultry and Egg Association: http://poultryegg.org
United Egg Producers: http://www.uepcertified.com/

Contains VIDEO: The Veal Farm: http://www.vealfarm.com
Contains VIDEO: "Dairy Farming Today":
http://www.dairyfarmingtoday.org

National Pork Producers Council:
http://www.nppc.org/public_policy/animal_health.html
National Pork Board: http://www.pork.org,
http://pork4kids.com/

National Cattleman's Association: http://beef.org and
http://www.beeffrompasturetoplate.org/animalwelfare.aspx

Advocates of non- factory-farm/intensive livestock
production:
Certified Humane: http://www.certifiedhumane.org
Animal Compassion Foundation:
http://www.animalcompassionfoundation.org

Some critics of animal agriculture:
Compassion Over Killing (http://cok.net): "Exposing routine
cruelty in the chicken industry":
http://www.chickenindustry.com/
Compassion Over Killing (http://cok.net): "Exposing the Truth
about Eggs," http://www.eggindustry.com/
Compassionate Consumers' film "Wegmans Cruelty":
http://WegmansCruelty.com
Farm Sanctuary (http://farmsanctuary.org):
http://factoryfarming.org
Farmed Animal Net: http://farmedanimal.net/ (news service)
HSUS: http://www.hsus.org/farm_animals/
PETA: http://www.goveg.com/factoryFarming.asp
United Poultry Concerns: http://www.upc-online.org/
Vegan Outreach: http://www.veganoutreach.org/whyvegan/

On vegetarian and veganism:
American Dietetic Association's Position Paper on Vegetarian
Diets, *JADA*, June 2003 (Vol. 103, Issue 6, Pages 748-765):
http://www.eatright.org/cps/rde/xchg/ada/hs.xsl/advocacy_
933_ENU_HTML.htm Full article at
http://ethicsandanimals.googlepages.com/ada-veg.pdf
PCRM: http://pcrm.org/health/
COK's TryVeg.com page: http://www.tryveg.com

PETA's Go Veg page: http://GoVeg.com

Vegan Outreach's Vegan Health page:
http://www.veganhealth.org/

Peter Singer and Jim Mason, *The Way We Eat: Why Our Food Choices Matter* (Rodale, 2006). *A recent discussion of the many ethical issues raised by animal agriculture and an evaluation of a range of responses to the issues.*

Matthew Halteman, "Compassionate Eating as Care of Creation," on the intersection of animal ethics and faith issues (from a Christian perspective):
http://www.hsus.org/religion/resources/compassionate_eating_as_care_.html

Christian Vegetarian Association: http://www.all-creatures.org/cva/

Jewish Vegetarians: http://www.jewishveg.com/

Fur and Food

Philosophers often don't discuss the fur industry. However, the fur industry is huge. And many people who do not consider themselves strong animal advocates claim to oppose it. If we ask them why they oppose it, however, they often give reasons that *seem* to imply that killing animals for food is also wrong. Yet these same people often resist that conclusion. Their choice, if they wish to remain consistent then, is to revise their view about the fur industry, revise their view about the meat, dairy and egg industries, or find a relevant different between the fur and agriculture industries such that one is wrong and the other is not. Can they do it?

Personal Challenges and Logic

In my 10 or so years' experience of teaching ethics courses, I have found that no topic brings out the rational and emotional *best* and *worst* in people than ethical questions about wearing and eating animals. This is not surprising since, unlike questions what *other people* should do, moral questions about animals are *personal*. As philosopher Peter Singer has observed, "For most human beings, especially in modern urban and suburban communities, the most direct form of contact with non-human animals is at mealtimes: we eat them"[1] (and wear them). For most of us, then, our own behavior is challenged when we reflect on the reasons given to think that change is needed in our treatment of, and attitudes toward, animals. That the issue is personal presents unique challenges, and great opportunities, for intellectual and moral progress.

This Chapter we will examine the common assumption that there is nothing wrong with harming animals – causing them pain, suffering, and an early death – so they might be eaten and worn. Our method, useful for better understanding all ethical debates, is

---

[1] Peter Singer, *Animal Liberation*, 3rd Ed. (New York: HarperCollins Publishers, 2002), p. 95.

68

to identify unambiguous and precise moral conclusions and make all the reasons in favor of the conclusion explicit, leaving no assumption unstated. Especially important will be the third of the three rules (introduced in Chapter 1) for identifying and evaluating arguments:

1. Make the stated conclusion(s) and premise(s) *precise* in quantity: is something said to be true (or false) of *all* things (or people, or animals, etc.), or just *some* of them (and if so, which ones?)?
2. Clarify the intended meaning(s) of unclear or ambiguous words in conclusions or premises.
3. State (any) *assumed* premises so that the *complete* pattern of reasoning in an argument is displayed and it is clear how the stated premise(s) logically leads to the conclusion.

People often try to argue that killing animals to eat them is morally permissible by offering a quick premise like, "Meat tastes good," or "I've always eaten meat." They don't seem to realize that they *seem* to be assuming the premises *if something tastes good then its permissible to kill it to eat it* (what if babies tasted good?!) and *if you've always done some action then doing that action morally permissible*, another arguably false premise.

Harms to Animals (and Humans): The Facts

Why is the treatment of animals a moral issue? The simple answer is that animals are *harmed* by the practices required to bring them to our plates and put them on our backs, and harms need moral defense. This unit reviews the case for these industries being extremely harmful to animals and looks at the industries' response to these charges. Harms to humans from eating animals (or eating animals to excess) are also detailed. Consider the position statement on vegetarianism from the leading authority on nutrition in North America based on their sixteen-page review of the recent nutrition research:

It is the position of the American Dietetic Association that appropriately planned vegetarian diets, including total vegetarian or vegan diets, are healthful, nutritionally adequate, and may provide health benefits in the prevention and treatment of certain diseases. Well-planned vegetarian diets are appropriate for individuals during all stages of the life cycle, including pregnancy, lactation, infancy, childhood, and adolescence, and for athletes. . .. An evidence-based review showed that vegetarian diets can be nutritionally adequate in pregnancy and result in positive maternal and infant health outcomes. The results of an evidence-based review showed that a vegetarian diet is associated with a lower risk of death from ischemic heart disease. Vegetarians also appear to have lower low-density lipoprotein cholesterol levels, lower blood pressure, and lower rates of hypertension and type 2 diabetes than nonvegetarians. Furthermore, vegetarians tend to have a lower body mass index and lower overall cancer rates. Features of a vegetarian diet that may reduce risk of chronic disease include lower intakes of saturated fat and cholesterol and higher intakes of fruits, vegetables, whole grains, nuts, soy products, fiber, and phytochemicals.[1]

Ethical behavior *can* require self-sacrifice; however, this scientific research suggests that ethical behavior – i.e., *if* killing animals to eat them is wrong – *can* lead to personal health benefits.

Factory Farming vs. Vegetarianism vs. Veganism vs. "Humane" Animal Agriculture vs.??

To return to the first Chapter, we can envision Regan's "cat case" transformed into a fur-bearer and an animal farmed for food. Here are some of the options:

---

[1] "Position of the American Dietetic Association: Vegetarian Diets," *Journal of the American Dietetic Association*, 2009 Jul;109(7): 1266-82. http://www.eatrightpro.org/resource/practice/position-and-practice-papers/position-papers/vegetarian-diets

A. Any (or almost any) use of those animals is morally permissible; there are no moral obligations to those animals.

B. Seriously harming those animals (e.g., causing them pain and suffering, killing them, etc.) is morally permissible provided they are housed in comfortable cages.

C. Seriously harming those animals is permissible provided they are housed in comfortable cages, treated gently and killed painlessly.

D. Seriously harming those animals is typically morally wrong, *even if* they are housed in comfortable cages, treated gently and killed painlessly.

Option (C) is intended to be analogous to so-called "humane" animal farming and slaughter. While everyone agrees that this is better for animals than factory farming, the question still remains: is this treatment of animals is morally permissible or not? If something like option (D) is the most ethically defensible option, then (C) is not.

"Painless" and "Humane" Killing

Option (C) includes the often heard claim that, "if animals are killed painlessly, then that's morally OK." This assumption might be true, but it's worthwhile to notice that we reject it about ourselves. In most cases, if we were killed, even "painlessly," we would be deprived of our (hopefully valuable) futures: everything we would have experienced is taken from us. Insofar as animals have futures, and killing them prevents them from experiencing those futures (and any of the good experiences they would have had), it seems that the same basic reasons why it is wrong to kill us might apply to many animals. So the assumption that "painless killing is automatically morally permissible" should be, at least, strongly doubted: good reasons would need to be given its favor.

Discussion Questions

1. For many ethical issues, a good place to start is to reflect on "common views" about the issues. Suppose you surveyed a range of people and asked them whether it's morally permissible to wear and/or eat animals and *why*. What are some of the most common answers that would be given? What *reasons* would you often hear in favor of these answers? Are these reasons generally good reasons or not? Why?

2. Describe how animals are treated by the fur and animal agribusiness industries: what happens to animals when used for these purposes? What are the facts? How do these industries describe how they treat animals? Are they correct in their description of the facts?

3. Explain the strongest moral arguments for the conclusions that (a) it's wrong to kill animals for fur and/or the fur industry is morally impermissible and (b) it's wrong to raise and kill animals for meat, milk, and eggs and/or the animal agriculture industry – i.e., factory farming – is morally impermissible. Are these arguments sound or not? Explain and defend your views.

4. Explain the strongest and/or most common moral arguments for the conclusions that (a) *it's not wrong to kill animals for fur* and/or (b) *it's not wrong to raise and kill animals for meat, milk and eggs*. Are these arguments sound or not? Explain and defend your views.

5. Should people (at least in "modern," industrialized societies) be vegetarians? Or should they be vegans? Or should they support smaller-scale, non-industrial, so-called "humane" animal farming and slaughter? Or should they support factory farming? Explain which response best captures our moral obligations and why.

Of course, always feel free to raise any other questions, observations, criticisms and any other responses to the Chapter's readings and issues.

Paper option

Write a 4-6 page argumentative essay that addresses all these questions and *defends* your answers from the strongest and/or most common objections:

- *In our society*, should animals and killed be raised to be eaten? What kind of treatment of farmed animals is morally permissible? Are there any changes that we are morally obligated to make regarding how chickens, pigs, cows and other (currently) farmed animals are treated? Defend your answers with reasons.

- *In our society*, should animals and killed be raised to be fur-trimmed and fur coats? What kind of treatment of fur-bearers is morally permissible? Are there any changes that we are morally obligated to make regarding how fur-bearers are treated? Defend your answers with reasons.

- What are the relationships between your answers about the fur and food animals issues, and your reasons in favor of these answers?

What should your personal response to these issues be? Should you buy or wear fur? Should you buy or eat meat, eggs and/or dairy products? If yes, from where? If no, why not?

CHAPTER 6: EXPERIMENTING ON ANIMALS; ANIMALS IN EDUCATION

Overview

This Chapter we will consider perhaps the most controversial ethical issues concerning animals, namely questions about the morality of animal experimentation and research for medical, scientific, psychological, educational and *veterinary* purposes. These issues are often considered most controversial because, unlike using animals for clothing, entertainment or even food, it is claimed that animal research provides *significant* medical benefits for humans that, some claim, *could not be attained any other way* than by using animals. Thus, this is an area where animals' and humans' interests are said to unavoidably conflict. This Chapter we will attempt to evaluate claims about the scientific and medical merit of animal experimentation, as these *might* be relevant to its morality (or the might not), and directly attempt to determine the morality of various kinds of animal use in science, medicine, education and research.

Readings

ANIMAL LIBERATION – 2. Tools for Research . . . *your taxes at work*

EMPTY CAGES – 10. Turning Animals into Tools

ANIMALS LIKE US – Ch. 6. Using Animals for Experiments

Gruen: 4. Animal research (optional)

"The Case for the Use of Animals in Biomedical Research," *New England Journal of Medicine*, http://ethicsandanimals.googlepages.com/cohen.pdf

Adrian Morrison; "Personal Reflections on the "Animal-Rights" Phenomenon": http://www.the-

aps.org/publications/tphys/2001html/February01/personal_r
eflections.htm; "First, animals aren't people" http://www.the-
aps.org/pa/action/charity/morrison.htm

Bob Speth, "Muddlers Beware: The Case for Philosophical
Extremism," (a review of Regan's *Empty Cages*) *Newsletter of the
Society for Veterinary Medical Ethics*, Volume 10, Number 3
October 2004, pp. 9-13; Regan's reply, pp. 14-18.
http://www.vetmed.wsu.edu/org_SVME/images/vol10-3.pdf

Charles Nicoll & Sharon Russell: selections at
http://ethicsandanimals.googlepages.com/nicoll%26russellona
nimalethics

Stuart Derbyshire, "The hard arguments about vivisection":
http://www.spiked-online.com/Articles/0000000CAFA7.htm

Jonathan Balcombe, "Dissection: The Scientific Case for
Alternatives," *Journal of Applied Animal Welfare Science*, (4), 2,
117-126, 2001.
http://ethicsandanimals.googlepages.com/balcombe.pdf
This article is a summary of Balcombe, J.P. (2000). *The Use of
Animals in Higher Education: Problems: Alternatives and
Recommendations.* Washington, DC: Humane Society
Press. http://www.hsus.org/press_and_publications/humane
_bookshelf/the_use_of_animals_in_higher_education_proble
ms_alternatives_and_recommendations.html

Recommended Reading & Viewing:
Some advocates of animal experimentation:
- *Americans for Medical Progress*:
  http://www.amprogress.org
- *Foundation for Biomedical Research*:
  http://www.fbresearch.org/
- *National Association for Biomedical Research*:
  http://www.nabr.org/

- *American Association for Laboratory Animal Science*
  http://www.aalas.org/

Some critics of animal experimentation:
 Scientific:

- *Americans For Medical Advancement*:
  http://curedisease.com
- *Physicians Committee for Responsible Medicine (PCRM):*
  http://pcrm.org/resch/
- *Medical Research Modernization Committee:*
  http://www.mrmcmed.org

Ethical:

- HSUS: http://www.hsus.org/animals_in_research/
- PETA: http://www.stopanimaltests.org
- AAVS: http://www.aavs.org/
- NEAVS: http://www.neavs.org/
- NAVS: http://www.navs.org

Science Does Not Answer Moral Questions

An important thing to remember in discussing the morality of animal experimentation is that *science does not answer moral questions*. What benefits (if any) that result from any kind of experiment (human or animal) do not *in themselves* show that some experiment is morally justified. That occurs only in conjunction with moral principles and moral reasons, and those aren't determined by the science. Making arguments logically valid can make this clear because then it will be obvious that there's a "leap" from some claim about benefits or scientific results to a, *therefore*, doing this is morally permissible. As stated, the conclusion does not yet follow.

Theoretical Foundations and Unprincipled Responses

One way of addressing moral questions it to appeal to moral principles and general theories of morality and moral reasoning: philosophers often approach issues that way, and so it is often clear what their moral arguments are and what reasons are given for their premises. Many defenders of animal experimentation do not follow this pattern however and so we must make premises and conclusions clear and precise and, if needed, add the missing premise(s) needed to reveal the full pattern of reasoning. Here are a number of common arguments given in defense of animal experimentation that should be addressed before we get to the readings:

"Benefits" Arguments

Many people argue that there are medical benefits for humans that result from animal experimentation, e.g., treatments and cures for diseases, improvements in health, and so forth – and that, therefore, animal experimentation is morally permissible. The suggested argument is this:

(P1) Animal experimentation benefits humans.
(C) Therefore, animal experimentation is morally permissible.

There are many problems with this argument. First, (P1) is imprecise in many ways. *Much* animal experimentation is done without *any* expectation that it will yield (medical) benefits for humans. So (P1) should claim that *some* animal experimentation benefits humans. But there is more imprecision. It either says:

(P2) Some animal experimentation benefits *some* humans,

or

(P3) Some animal experimentation benefits *all* humans.

(P3) is false. About 30,000 people, many of whom are children, die *each day* from starvation, malnutrition, and lack of *very basic* medical care.[1] These people, and at least millions of other humans, do not benefit from it. About (P2), *as it is stated*, few scientific, humanistic and/or ethical critics of animal experimentation deny it. There have been many, many experiments on animals. To claim that *not one* of them has led to *any* benefits for *any* humans – even just by good luck – would be to claim something false. So (P2) *is* true: *some* humans benefit medically from *some* animal experimentation. Some people seem to think this *automatically* shows that animal experimentation is morally permissible. Oddly, they often seem to think this supports a more precise conclusion that *all* animal experiments are permissible, even those that do not lead to any benefits for humans and are expected not to. But no such conclusions follow, for many reasons. First, just because *some* humans benefit from something does not entail that it is morally permissible for them to get it: e.g., some people might benefit from an *extremely* expensive medical procedure, or from receiving vital organs taken from living, healthy people. But those benefits

---

[1] Peter Singer's *One World: The Ethics of Globalization* (Yale, 2002) provides information and arguments for the conclusion that we are morally obligated to assist people in absolute poverty. See also *his The Life You Can Save* and more recent books on absolute poverty: http://www.thelifeyoucansave.org

do not *automatically* justify directing so much money toward them (at the expense of others) or killing innocent people to take those organs.

To assume something different about animal cases – i.e., that it is morally permissible to seriously harm animals to benefit humans – just *assumes* that animal experimentation is permissible: it does not give any reasons in favor of that. As we saw above, common claims about rights, importance, and moral status do not justify this assumption, but perhaps arguments discussed below will help justify it.

"Necessity" Arguments

Related to the argument from benefits is the argument from "necessity" or the claim that animal experiments are "essential": "animal experiments are 'necessary'; therefore, they are morally permissible." To evaluate this argument, we must first ask what is *meant* by "necessary"? There is a sense of the term on which animal experimentation clearly *is* necessary: to do experiments on animals, it is *necessary* to do experiments on animals. This is true because to do any exact, particular action, it is *necessary* to do *that* action. Whatever is truly meant by "necessity," an advocate of these arguments assumes a moral premise like the following:

> *If* doing some action is "necessary," *then* it is morally permissible.

For some meanings of "necessity" animal experimentation advocates attach to that claim, it will likely be false to say that all, or even much, animal experimentation is "necessary." For these meanings, this moral principle will have no application. There are other meanings of "necessary," e.g., that to say something is "necessary" could be to say that, "it couldn't be achieved in any other way." On this meaning, many animal experiments *are* "necessary." But, on this meaning, some human vivisection is also "necessary" since some benefits from it also "cannot be achieved in any other way." The principle above implies such vivisection is not wrong, but it is, so the above principle is arguably false.

"No Alternatives" Arguments

The same critical observations can be given about arguments from there allegedly being "no alternatives" to animal experimentation: that's likely false and that doesn't seem to automatically make doing something morally permissible either.

"Painless" and "Humane" Killing, Again

In the context of experimentation, we also hear the "if the animals are killed painlessly, then that's morally OK" assumption. Again, we should notice that we reject it about ourselves. In most cases, if we were killed, even "painlessly," we would be deprived of our (hopefully valuable) futures: everything we would have experienced is taken from us. Insofar as animals have futures, and killing them prevents them from experiencing those futures (and any of the good experiences they would have had), it seems that the same basic reasons why it is wrong to kill us apply to many animals. So the assumption that "painless killing is automatically morally permissible" should be, at least, strongly doubted: good reasons would need to be given its favor.

Logic and Keeping Cool

While animal ethics, especially about animal experimentation and related issues, can be a heated topic, logic can help keep you cool. Find conclusions, ask for reasons, and demand a fair and impartial evaluation of those reasons. Keep the ethics and the science straight, and remember that scientific results have moral implications only in light of moral principles. By taking this course, you have more "ethics training" than nearly all scientists who defend animal use, so make use of your skills!

Discussion Questions

1. For many ethical issues, a good place to start is to reflect on "common views" about the issues. Suppose you surveyed a range of people and asked them whether it's morally permissible (or even morally obligatory) to experiment on animals and *why*. What are some of the most common answers that would be given? What *reasons* would you often hear in favor of these answers? Are these reasons generally good reasons or not? Why?
2. Describe how animals are treated by in medical, scientific, psychological, educational and industrial experimentation and research: what happens to animals when used for these purposes? What are the facts? How do these industries describe how they treat animals? Are they correct in their description of the facts?
3. Explain the strongest moral arguments for the conclusions that animal experimentation is (nearly always) wrong *and/or* that an experiment on an animal is wrong *unless* the experimenters would be willing to perform the experiment on a similarly conscious and sentient human infant. Are these arguments sound or not? Explain and defend your views.
4. Summarize the wide range of activities and methods of research that can be (and is) done to improve human health and cure disease that does not involve animals.
5. Explain the strongest and/or most common moral arguments for the conclusions that (a) animal experimentation is almost never wrong, indeed it's often morally obligatory and/or (b) animal experimentation is morally justified when it is "necessary" because there are "no alternatives" to produce the desired benefits. Are these arguments sound or not? Explain and defend your views.

Of course, always feel free to raise any other questions, observations, criticisms and any other responses to the Chapter's readings and issues.

Paper option

What, if any, kind of medical, scientific, psychological, commercial/industrial, educational and/or *veterinary* experimentation or research (and other uses, e.g., dissections) are morally permissible? Which are morally impermissible? Thoroughly defend your view and respond to the strongest and/or most common objections to your arguments. 4-6 pages.

CHAPTER 7: PETS / COMPANION ANIMALS; ZOOS, HUNTING, RACING, AND OTHER USES OF ANIMALS

Overview

This chapter we will discuss the moral responsibilities involved in keeping pets or companion animals and related moral issues concerning shelters, adoption, and killing unwanted companion animals. We will also discuss the arguments for and against hunting, dog and horse racing, rodeos, zoos and related uses of animals: is using animals for any or all of these purposes morally permissible or not? Why or why not?

Readings

EMPTY CAGES – 8. Turning Animals into Performers

ANIMALS LIKE US – Ch. 7. Zoos

EMPTY CAGES – 9. Turning Animals into Competitors

ANIMALS LIKE US – Ch. 8. Hunting
ANIMALS LIKE US – Ch. 9. Pets

Gruen: 5. Dilemmas of captivity and 6. Animals in the wild (optional)

Keith Burgess-Jackson, "Doing Right by Our Animal Companions" in David Benatar, ed., *Ethics for Everyday* (McGraw-Hill, 2002),
http://ethicsandanimals.googlepages.com/kbj-pets.pdf

Gary Varner, "Pets, Companion Animals, and Domesticated Partners," in David Benatar, ed., *Ethics for Everyday* (McGraw-Hill, 2002), pp. 150-75
http://philosophy.tamu.edu/~gary/Publications/ using "guest" and "enter" when prompted for an ID and a password, respectively.

Further Reading:

- Association of Zoos and Aquariums: http://www.aza.org/
- Ringling Brothers' circus: http://www.ringling.com/animals/
- Search these animal groups' pages about these issues: HSUS: http://www.hsus.org/ (http://www.hsus.org/wildlife/issues_facing_wildlife/circuses/), PETA: http://www.peta.org/ (www.circuses.com)

"Pets" & Pet "Ownership" vs. Companion Animals & Animal Guardians

Keeping animals as companions raises unique responsibilities. Unlike many other ethical issues involving animals where our moral obligations are arguably largely "negative" – to *not* harm them, to leave them alone, etc. – we arguably have "positive" obligations towards any companion animals we might bring into our homes, e.g., to provide them with food, shelter, medical care, and companionship. This, of course, takes time, effort and money, sometimes a lot of money.

These financial demands can be a burden and give rise to hard questions about the extent of our obligations to animals. After all, there is no health insurance for animals, and animals' healthcare costs could create great financial strain. What should be done in these common situations? Go into debt to pay for the medical bills? Find someone else to take the animal who can pay? Have the animal killed? Something else? The answers might not be morally or financially easy.

Many critics of animal advocates often say things like, "Animal rights advocates oppose having pets." This claim seems to be a result either of ignorance or intentional manipulation. First, many animal advocates, including philosophers, have companion animals and often mention these animals in their writings. So it is ignorant to claim that animals advocates oppose having animals as companions.

Many animal advocates, however, do oppose companion animal *ownership* and, perhaps, the use of the word "pet" if it implies ownership. This is because if you own something, then that something is your *property*. And (generally, with some exceptions), if something is your property, then (generally, with some exceptions) you can do *whatever you want with it*, including destroy (or kill) it for whatever reason you would like, or no reason at all. Thus, the objection is that in thinking of companion animals as pets and thereby owned property, that nearly implies that animals' interests deserve no consideration in their own right and so on. Animal advocates, of course, reject that. And they argue that breeding companion animals is wrong because for every "new" animal produced another already existing animal in a shelter will not be adopted and thus killed. But they also believe that animals, such as cats and dogs, can be kept as companions, provided they are well cared for.

These are some common views about companion animals held by many animal advocates. Given that this is what they believe, why do critics of animal advocacy so often say that animal advocates oppose keeping companion animals?

Ends and Means

Like many uses of animals, using animals in rodeos, circuses, zoos, racing, in hunting, etc. are often justified by appealing to various "ends" or "products" of the use. For these kinds of arguments (for both these issues, as well as when this kind of argument is used to defend eating animals, or experimenting on them, and so on), here are some questions to ask:

- Is this a morally justified end, i.e., some worthy goal?
    - E.g., zoos might be justified by the claim that they are supposed to result in *greater respect for animals*, arguably a laudable goal. Rodeos might be justified by the claim that they produce *entertainment for people*, surely a more controversial goal. Some hunters might claim that the goal of hunting is *to bring about the human pleasures resulting from killing animals*, arguably a goal that could not be morally justified.
- Is this use of animals an *effective*, or the most effective, means toward that goal?
    - E.g., with zoos, scientific research might show that zoo attendance results in no greater respect for animals, and perhaps increased disrespect for animals. Thus, perhaps zoos are not an effective means toward that end. Regarding hunting, yes, killing animals is indeed the most effective means to getting the pleasures that people claim to get from killing animals (but perhaps video games could have similar results?).

- Or are there other, better, ways to achieve this goal?
  - E.g., regarding zoos, surely there are better ways to teach respect for animals. Regarding rodeos, there are other ways to produce entertainment for humans and, arguably, ways that don't produce harm for animals (or humans) surely are morally better than those that depend on harm.
- Finally, what exactly are the *best* reasons to think that using animals for such an end is *morally justified*, especially in cases where animals are harmed greatly (and we would never dream of using human beings for such a purpose)? Are these reasons any good, i.e., sound arguments for the conclusion that this activity is morally permissible? And what exactly are the *best* reasons to think that using animals for such an end is *morally unjustified*, especially in cases where animals are harmed greatly (and we would never dream of using human beings for such a purpose)?

These sorts of questions above are applicable to all questions about animal use.

Discussion Questions

1. For many ethical issues, a good place to start is to reflect on "common views" about the issues. Suppose you surveyed a range of people and asked them about the morality of the various uses of animals in this unit. What are some of the most common answers that would be given? What *reasons* would you often hear in favor of these answers? Are these reasons generally good reasons or not? Why?
2. While some critics of animal advocates claim that animal advocates *oppose* keeping "pets" or companion animals, they are clearly mistaken and ignorant of what animal advocates think. Nevertheless, what ethical issues and responsibilities are raised by keeping pets or companion animals? Are any issues genuinely challenging? Morally,

how should we respond to these issues?

3. Describe how animals are treated by the various industries discussed in this unit and used in these various ways: what happens to animals when used for these purposes? What are the facts? How do these industries and practitioners describe how they treat animals? Are they correct in their description of the facts?

4. Explain the strongest moral arguments *in favor of* using animals for entertainment, for zoos, for hunting, and/or any other uses from this section. Are these arguments sound or not? Explain and defend your views.

5. Explain the strongest moral arguments *against* using animals for entertainment, for zoos, for hunting, and/or any other uses from this section. Are these arguments sound or not? Explain and defend your views.

Of course, always feel free to raise any other questions, observations, criticisms and any other responses to the Chapter's readings and issues.

Paper option

Write a 4-6 page argumentative essay that explains and addresses the ethical issues raised by at least one of the uses of animals discussed in the readings this Chapter, defend a moral conclusion about that issue, and respond to the strongest and/or most common objections to your arguments.

CHAPTER 8: ACTIVISM FOR ANIMALS

Overview

What, if any, kinds of actions done to try to improve the treatment of animals (including, perhaps, trying to eliminate various uses of animals) are morally permissible? Which, if any, are morally obligatory? Changing our diets? Educating others? Working for larger cages and more humane treatment, or for the abolishment of (some) animal use industries, or *both*? Trying to change the laws to better protect animals? Illegal actions (done covertly or openly)? Undercover investigations to reveal animal abuse? Rescuing or releasing animals from animal use industries? Exposing people and businesses who support harmful animal use? Violence of any kind, ever? Threats of violence? *Terrorism*? We will explore a range of tactics and attempt to evaluate them morally.

Readings

EMPTY CAGES – PART V – MANY HANDS ON MANY OARS
EMPTY CAGES – 11. "Yes . . . but . . ."
EMPTY CAGES – EPILOGUE – The Cat

ANIMAL LIBERATION – 6. Speciesism Today . . . defenses, rationalizations, and objections to Animal Liberation and the progress made in overcoming them Also re-read the 2002 Preface to Animal Liberation.

ANIMALS LIKE US – Ch. 10. Animal Rights Activism
ANIMALS LIKE US – Ch. 11. What Goes Around Comes Around

Gruen: 7. Protecting animals. (optional)

Matt Ball, *Vegan Outreach*, "Working in Defense of Animals"
http://www.veganoutreach.org/enewsletter/20030105.html
Vegan Outreach "Adopt a College" Program:

http://www.veganhealth.org/colleges/

Bruce Friedrich (PETA), "Effective Advocacy: Stealing from the Corporate Playbook"
http://www.goveg.com/effectiveAdvocacy.asp

Karen Dawn, about Dawnwatch:
http://dawnwatch.com/introduction.htm

James LaVeck (Tribe of Heart film production company), "Invasion of the Movement Snatchers: A Social Justice Cause Falls Prey to the Doctrine of "Necessary Evil"
http://www.tribeofheart.org/tohhtml/essay_ims.htm (see his other essays as well)
Gary Francione, "The Abolition of Animal Exploitation: The Journey Will Not Begin While We Are Walking Backwards,"
http://www.abolitionist-online.com/article-issue05_gary.francione_abolition.of.animal.exploitation.2006.s html

The Center for Consumer Freedom: http://www.activistcash.com/ & http://www.consumerfreedom.com/
SourceWatch on the Activist Cash page
http://www.sourcewatch.org/index.php?title=A_visit_to_the_ActivistCash.com_web_site and the Center for Consumer Freedom:
http://www.sourcewatch.org/index.php?title=Center_for_Consumer_Freedom

Wikipedia entry on the Animal Liberation Front:
http://en.wikipedia.org/wiki/Animal_Liberation_Front

Recommended Reading:
- Peter Singer, ed. *In Defense of Animals: The Second Wave* (Blackwell)
- Steve Best, ed., *Terrorists or Freedom Fighters? Reflections on the Liberation of Animals* (Lantern).

Criticisms or Complaints about (Some) Activists Have No Implications for the Morality of Animal Use

Activists try to bring about change in others' beliefs, attitudes and behavior. Naturally, since people tend to be resistant to change, people often do not like activists. This dislike sometimes leads to bad arguments.

When people are unhappy with activists and what they do, they sometimes seem to think that this has some bearing on the morality of the *actions* that that the activist is concerned with. For example, you might hear someone say something like, "It's OK to eat meat. After all, vegetarians are so pushy and self-righteous and 'in your face' about it all." Or, "Animal research is clearly a good thing. After all, animal rights activists are so obnoxious in their protests and some of them even break the law and try to intimidate scientists." Activists – for animals and many other issues – often get called a lot of bad names and are thought poorly of.

These responses, while unfortunately common, are extremely poor, if they are given to try to show that some use of animals is, contrary to what the activist argues, morally permissible. This is because no moral evaluation of *actions* follows from evaluations about *people*. Think about the abortion controversy. Suppose someone said, "Some anti-abortionists threaten and even murder abortion providers; these activists are bad people." If they then said, "*Therefore*, we should think that abortion is morally OK," the conclusion simply doesn't follow. And it never follows elsewhere: whether an action is morally permissible or not is not determined by any activists' behavior, good or bad. The issues are separate and logically distinct.

"Smear campaigns" against activists are also typically based on false generalizations about activists. Yes, *some* animal activists are rude, obnoxious or whatever, but surely *some* animal use advocates are also rude, obnoxious or whatever. And some animal advocates are also quite nice, friendly and respectful, as are some advocates of animal use (at least to human beings). But we must keep in mind that none of this has any bearing on the moral status of any animal use.

"Welfarism" & "Welfarists" versus "Animal Rights" & "Abolitionists": Ends and Means

A current heated controversy among animal advocates is whether they should be – as some describe it – *either* advocates of "animal welfare" and "welfare reforms," *or* advocates for "animal rights" and the "abolition" of harmful animal use or *both*. These terms are often ill-defined and not carefully thought through. This can lead to needless conflict among animal advocates and an inability to understand what kind of information might help resolve these debates. Thinking about "ends" or "goals" and "means" or "strategies" can help us understand these distinctions and better assess (and perhaps *overcome*) this debate amongst activists.

First, ends: what would be a morally acceptable *end goal* for the treatment of animals? What kind of world would we have if all animals were treated in morally permissible ways, where we could say, "We have achieved the moral goal for how animals ought to be treated since none are treated wrongly anymore?"

Regan's cat case presents two broad options – among many – for such a goal:

C. Seriously harming animals is permissible provided they are housed in comfortable cages, treated gently and killed painlessly.

D. Seriously harming animals is typically morally wrong, *even if* they are housed in comfortable cages, treated gently and killed painlessly.

Anyone who claims (C) is an acceptable goal or end we can call a "welfarist": they believe that once *certain kinds* of harms to animals are minimized or eliminated, it is still usually morally permissible to seriously harm animals, e.g., by killing them. Their view might vary depending on the purposes behind these harms, of course. And there are important details, e.g., about which harms are permissible to cause and which aren't, that they would need to explain so we fully understand the view. And, most importantly, whether any arguments in favor of welfarism are sound and withstand objections is something we would want to think about very carefully.[1]

Anyone who believes that (C) is deficient for an ideal goal and that (D) is that ideal we might call a "genuine" animal rights advocate. Or, so that we say what we really mean, we could just say they believe that *seriously harming animals is typically morally wrong, even if they are housed in comfortable cages, treated gently and killed painlessly.* We would want to understand their reasons for why they think that, and whether any arguments in favor of this kind of view are sound and withstand critical scrutiny is something we would also want to think about very carefully.

Beyond the question of acceptable or ideal final goals or ends for animals is the question of "means": what sort of actions, policies, strategies, campaigns, and other activist activities will be the most effective *means* toward the desired end goal for animals? In particular, if the goal is (D), the "animal rights" end, what should be done *now* to best achieve this, or get us closest to it, as soon as possible?

Here is where the debate begins. Should we now campaign for larger cages, and, once successful with that, then campaign for "no cages" – i.e., argue that animals shouldn't be used in the first place? (Or should some activists do the former and other activists the latter?) The former *might* lead to some small improvements now (or it might not), but it also might forestall or prevent greater improvements that *might* have occurred had the focus been on "empty cages." On the other hand, campaigns for "empty cages" *might* fall on too many deaf ears and yield no short term

---

[1] Some might observe that, in practice, those who call themselves "welfarists" or "advocates of animal welfare" typically accept just about any use of animals, i.e., they deem just about all harmful uses of animals as "necessary" and/or respecting "animal welfare." This may be true, but it doesn't show that welfarism is false. This may, however, suggest that there really is no clearly defined view "welfarism": it's just some words that people use but the view really has no implications for animal use because we can't pin it down in any rigorous way. See Gary Francione's writings for discussion (Google).

improvements. But perhaps enough ears eventually will hear the message and this will result in widespread *abolition* of animal use, perhaps incrementally, one industry or sub-industry after another. Or maybe not.

These debates are often divisive, but it's not clear that they should be. For one, they often involve matters that are largely speculative, such as the long-term effects of some campaign strategy (as compared to another). Here we are dealing with little knowledge and hard data; we are often left with guesswork, hopes and under-informed estimations. This ignorance should result in greater humility and less dogmatism on this topic, and a call for *formal* training in areas that might bring in some useful information to help us answer these questions about means, such as economics, marketing, consumer psychology, statistics and so forth. We should agree that we don't know what we need to know to bring about our desired end, and turn our focus towards gaining that knowledge.

A second reason why these debates shouldn't be divisive is that it is not clear that they are philosophical ones. As suggested above, they are largely empirical and scientific. Our ends do not obviously dictate our means. Suppose we lived a few hundred years ago, came to believe that slavery was wrong and should be abolished, not merely made more "humane." We have set our *ends*, but what *means* should we use to achieve that end ASAP? Back then, there was no obvious answer, for reasons comparable to those mentioned about. These issues were debated then (and are still debated now, since human slavery still exists) and animal advocates can surely learn from studying that debate.

Animal Advocates *Promoting* Animal Use?

As a concrete example of the issue above, some animal advocacy organizations have recently begun giving a "platform" for animal-use industries, especially those who practice so-called "humane" farming. Whether this is an effective (or dismal) strategic means to help bring about an "animal rights" end, or whether this should be seen as a statement that the morally acceptable end really is "welfarism" is something that many activists have begun debating.

Illegal Actions

Let us now turn to some more controversial forms of activism. Consider "open rescues" of animals from farms: these typically involve *trespass, breaking and entering,* and *theft* of animals that are somebody's *property.* All these actions are *illegal.* Some people argue that *such rescues are morally wrong because they are illegal.* They might argue similarly against any form of activism that involves illegal activity.

These are unsound arguments and nearly everyone agrees with that because nearly everyone believes that this unstated premise, which is essential to the argument, is *false*:

> Necessarily, if an action is illegal, then it is morally impermissible.

Hiding Jews from Nazi's was illegal, yet morally permissible; helping slaves escape to freedom was illegal, yet morally permissible. Many more examples make the same point. Contrary to a common reaction, these examples *do not* make *any* "comparisons" *whatsoever* between animal issues and slavery or human holocausts[1]; they are simply used to show that any (or just about any) argument against some kind of activism based on the premise that it is illegal is unsound (or, at least, just about everyone's beliefs entail that it is unsound, since they think the above premise is false: just because something is illegal does not necessarily entail that it is morally wrong). Animal advocates are advised to read Martin Luther King, Jr.'s 1963 "Letter from a Birmingham Jail."[2] They will find much to resonate with Dr. King's discussion.

---

[1] For an insightful discussion of such comparisons, see Karen Davis's *The Holocaust and the Henmaid's Tale: A Case for Comparing Atrocities* (Lantern, 2005). http://www.upc-online.org/

[2] Widely reposted online; http://www.stanford.edu/group/King/frequentdocs/birmingham.pdf

Violent Actions

More controversial forms of activism involve violence or threats of violence of different kinds. Violence comes in many different forms, as our authors observe.

Some animal advocates, e.g., some members of the ALF (Animal Liberation Front), engage in property destruction (e.g., of animal cages, computers with experimental data, etc.) and even sometimes even arson. Although they claim that their actions are "non-violent," this strains the concept of violence. They argue that since they are not violent *to* anyone, i.e., they do not inflict bodily harm on anyone, they thereby act non-violently.

This inference does not follow: one can act *violently* yet do no violence *to* anyone. For example, it seems to make perfect sense to say that someone could *violently* smash carton of fruits and vegetables with a sledgehammer, especially if the person was in a heated frenzy. One might not want young children to see such a spectacle because, well, it's too violent! So the ALF's insistence that they are always non-violent strains the meaning of the term. Perhaps they (and animal use industries) want to insist that they are non-violent because they think this principle is true:

All acts of violence are morally impermissible.

If this were true, and they acted violently (in performing arson, or in how they treat animals, for example), that would imply that they were acting wrongly.

But the above principle is false, according to most people: violence can be, and often is, morally justified. If violence (or threats of violence) are needed for self-defense, then it's permissible. If it's needed to defend an innocent third party, then it's justified. Perhaps some wars can be justified. So the above principle is false, according to most people.

Most people might even think that it's false regarding some animals too: if someone tried to attack your dog or cat, might you be morally justified in responding with violence, or threats of violence, to defend your companion animal if needed? What if the animal was a stray? What if the animal was in a farm, slaughterhouse or lab? If they knew the details of the case, perhaps many people might think that violence, if needed for defending animals, would be morally permissible in at least some of these cases.

So *perhaps* violence could be justified in cases of rescue. Whether violence can ever be justified for any other purposes, e.g., in an attempt to change society's general views about our obligations to animals, seems extremely doubtful. In fact, given all the relevant considerations, it is likely that any such violence, including possible *genuine* "terrorism," would be deeply morally wrong, for reasons that Regan, Singer and Rowlands articulate.

Discussion Questions

1. For many ethical issues, a good place to start is to reflect on "common views" about the issues. Suppose you surveyed a range of people and asked them what kinds of animal advocacy (if any) is good, effective and/or acceptable, and what kinds (if any) are bad, ineffective and/or unacceptable. What are some of the most common answers that would be given? What *reasons* would you often hear in favor of these answers? Are these reasons generally good reasons or not? Why?
2. Describe the range of options for activism for animals. Explain which you think are most effective or useful (for what?), the least effective or useful (for what?) and why.
3. Obviously, animal use industries are critical of animal activists. Describe their responses to activists, their "counter-activism" and your moral evaluation of their tactics.
4. Is any *illegal* activity (e.g., "open-rescues") for animals ever moral justified? When and why, or why not? Is violence, of any kind, ever morally justified? When and why, or why not?
5. What kind of activism, if any, should you personally be engaged in? Is this a moral obligation? Why should you do this kind activism rather than another? Justify your choices with reasons.

Of course, always feel free to raise any other questions, observations, criticisms and any other responses to the Chapter's readings and issues.

Paper option

A paper on activism: what kinds of activism (if any) are permissible? What (if any) are obligatory? What (if any) are wrong?

RECOMMENDED FURTHER READING:

Overviews of Animals & Ethics

1. Susan Armstrong & Richard Botzler, eds. *The Animal Ethics Reader*, 2nd Ed. (Routledge, 2003, 2008) is the only comprehensive anthology of ethics & animals writings currently available. It is less than ideal, however, because the pro-animal theoretical selections are perhaps not ideal (e.g., the selections from Singer and Regan are not the best available; the selections from other pro-animal ethical theoreticians are a bit idiosyncratic); there are few criticisms of pro-animal moral theorizing, little anti-animal ethical theorizing, and few defenses of particular animal uses; furthermore, the selection on animal experimentation is sparse. The strengths seem to be in the areas of wildlife and environmental issues, as those seem to be the editors' specialties.

2. Tom Regan and Carl Cohen, *The Animal Rights Debate* (Rowman & Littlefield, 2001) and Tom Regan, *Animal Rights, Human Wrongs: An Introduction to Moral Philosophy* (Rowman & Littlefield, 2003) (which is mostly The Animal Rights Debate minus Cohen's contribution) are great introductions: the latter argues for moral rights for animals (and humans) by examining competing moral theories. Regan's *The Case for Animal Rights* (University of California, 1983/2004) was recently reissued as a 20th anniversary edition with an updated preface containing replies to critics.

3. Tom Regan and Peter Singer, eds., Animal Rights and Human Obligations, 2nd ed. (Prentice Hall, 1989). An excellent collection, despite its age, but is *very expensive* ($75 new, but much cheaper used).

4. Bernard Rollin, *Animal Rights and Human Morality*, 3rd Ed. (Prometheus, 2006, 1998, 1981). Rollin is a philosopher who has interacted with tens of thousands of people employed in animal agribusiness and experimentation and so has a unique and valuable perspective on the issues. His

book is written in a personal style, with many anecdotes about his experiences.

5. Angus Taylor, *Animals and Ethics: An Overview of the Philosophical Debate, 3rd edition* (Broadview 2009). A nice overview of the literature. (On Amazon.)
6. Clare Palmer, "Animals in Anglo-American Philosophy" http://www.h-net.org/~animal/ruminations_palmer.html
7. Scott Wilson, "Animals and Ethics," *The Internet Encyclopedia of Philosophy* http://www.iep.utm.edu/a/anim-eth.htm
8. Lori Gruen, "The Moral Status of Animals," *The Stanford Encyclopedia of Philosophy*, http://plato.stanford.edu/entries/moral-animal/

On argument analysis

9. Richard Feldman's (University of Rochester, Philosophy) *Reason and Argument* text, 2nd Ed. (Prentice Hall, 1998
10. Nathan Nobis & Scott McElreath, *Making Moral Progress: An Ethical Arguments Workbook*, www.MakingMoralProgress.com (in progress)

On ethics

11. James Fieser, "Ethics," *The Internet Encyclopedia of Philosophy* (sections 2 and 3, on Normative Ethics and Applied Ethics are most relevant): http://www.iep.utm.edu/e/ethics.htm

On Animal Minds / Cognitive Ethology

12. Colin Allen (http://mypage.iu.edu/~colallen/), "Animal Consciousness," entry in Stanford Encyclopedia of Philosophy: http://plato.stanford.edu/entries/consciousness-animal/
13. Jonathan Balcombe, *Pleasurable Kingdom: Animals and The Nature of Feeling Good* (MacMillan 2006) http://www.pleasurablekingdom.com/
14. Marc Bekoff's web page and books: http://literati.net/Bekoff/

BONUS ESSAY: ABORTION AND ANIMAL RIGHTS: DOES EITHER TOPIC LEAD TO THE OTHER?[1]

Should your views on abortion influence your views on animal rights? Should your views on the moral status of animals influence your views on the moral status of human fetuses?

Generally, no. Most arguments against abortion have no implications for animal rights and those that might seem to be poor arguments against abortion. And arguments for animal rights only have implications for rare, later abortions of conscious fetuses, not the majority of abortions that affect early, pre-conscious fetuses.

On the other sides, though, a common of objection to animal rights does support a pro-life view and an influential feminist pro-choice argument does suggest positive implications for animals, though.

Overall, the topic of abortion presents with an inherent complexity never analogously present in animal rights issues – the perspective of the pregnant woman whose life and body the fetus depends on – and so the issues are importantly distinct.

Should people who believe in animal rights think that abortion is wrong? Should pro-lifers accept animal rights? If you think it's wrong to kill fetuses to end pregnancies, should you also think it's wrong to kill animals to, say, eat them? If you, say, oppose animal research, should you also oppose abortion?

Some argue 'yes' and others argue 'no' to either or both sets of questions.[1] The correct answer, however, seems to be, 'it depends': it depends on why someone accepts animal rights, and why someone thinks abortion is wrong: it depends on their reasons.

---

[1] Originally published (7/16/16) at *What's Wrong? The Blog of the University of Colorado, Boulder, Center for Values and Social Policy*: https://whatswrongcvsp.com/2016/07/16/whats-wrong-with-linking-abortion-and-animal-rights/

1. Animal Rights and Abortion Wrongs?

On some reasons, there is a clear connection between the topics.

If someone says abortion is wrong because fetuses are "**living things**," or "**organisms**," or "**beings**," those reasons clearly apply to animals, since they too are living things, organisms and beings. If someone else says animals have (moral) rights because they are living, organisms or beings, those reasons apply to human fetuses: they are alive (abortion involves killing them, and you can't kill non-living things), they are organisms (they are complex and developing) and they are beings (albeit dependent beings).

These arguments connect the topics: one argument leads to comparable conclusions for the other. If you think fetuses have rights, for those reasons, you should be inclined to think the same about animal rights, and vice versa.

These arguments are no good though. They both assume the premise that *all living things, organisms and/or beings are wrong to kill.* And that's not true. Plants, mold, bacteria and many insects, like mosquitoes and gnats are not wrong to kill, at least.

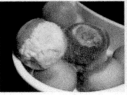

These types of things aren't even what's called "***prima facie***" wrong to kill, meaning something like, "Wrong to kill unless there is a very good reason to kill it." We, readers of this essay, are *prima facie* wrong to kill: if someone kills us, that's wrong unless there's a really good reason that justifies it. You don't need a *really good*

reason to kill a weed or a carrot, or some mold in your shower or a mosquito flying by.

So, these arguments connect the issues, but aren't good arguments about either: one didn't provide good reason to think that animals have rights, and the other doesn't provide good reason to think that abortion is wrong.

2. Abortion Wrongs and Animal Rights?

Let's consider some other arguments to seek a connection.

Let's start with abortion and see what might lead us to animal rights. Considering why abortion might be *prima facie* wrong is useful since most people who claim that abortion is wrong deny that is *absolutely* or *necessarily* wrong: they acknowledge some cases where it is not wrong: to save the life of the pregnant woman and perhaps rape, at least. So even people who call themselves "pro-life" typically think abortion is *prima facie* wrong. But why? And what might their reasons suggest for whether animals have rights?

Abortion is sometimes said to be prima facie wrong simply because fetuses are **human**. If 'human' means, ***biologically human*** then that argument just isn't going to apply to non-human animals, whether it's a good argument against abortion or not. And it's not: random biologically human cells and tissues are not even *prima facie* wrong to kill either: it wouldn't be wrong to kill a smear of living human cheek cells cultivated in a petri dish, for example.

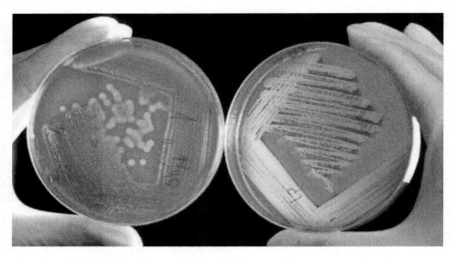

A more sophisticated argument is that abortion is prima facie wrong because fetuses are *biologically human organisms*: they are not random clumps of cells, but special cells that can develop into someone much like us (and so, some argue, they are someone like us now). Another argument is that abortion is prima facie wrong because fetuses are the "kind" of being that is a *rational moral agent*: a feline or bovine fetus, in contrast, is not that "kind" of being.

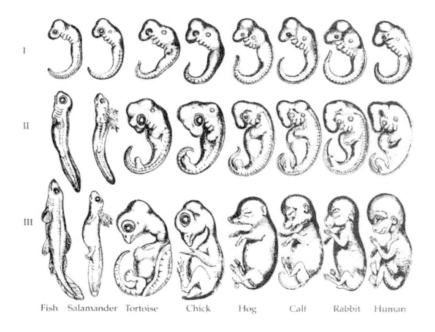

Fish Salamander Tortoise Chick Hog Calf Rabbit Human

Deciding whether these arguments are good or not requires some careful thinking. We can avoid that for now since these arguments don't connect the topics: non-human animals are not biologically human organisms and they likely are not rational moral agents or that "kind" of being. No argument that restricts serious moral concern only to humans or their unique abilities will connect to non-humans.

Another argument begins with the safe assumption that it is wrong to kill and act violently towards **innocent and vulnerable beings**. Since fetuses are innocent and vulnerable, killing them by abortion is wrong, so some argue.

This argument seems to apply to many animals, who are clearly innocent and vulnerable. Farm animals fearfully trying to escape from workers trying to kill them are clearly vulnerable beings: they are vulnerable to all sorts of physical and emotional harms. If this argument inclines anyone to think that the abuse of vulnerable and innocent animals is wrong and should stop, more power to it. (Some "pro-lifers" might resist though, claiming that their serious moral concern is only for innocent and vulnerable *human* life, not any and all innocent and vulnerable lives, not all victims of violence. We must ask what, if anything, might justify this speciesist prejudice, and that might be a long conversation, and we might conclude that this is an unjustified prejudice. But, we should notice that this new argument about abortion – now only concerning innocent, vulnerable *humans* – no longer has implications for non-human animals: it doesn't connect the topics.)

While it is true that innocent and vulnerable beings should be protected – that's a moral near-certainty – are fetuses really innocent and vulnerable, despite what people often say?

"**Innocent**" seems to mean something like "capable of intentionally doing wrong, but not doing wrong and so not deserving ill treatment." But fetuses, especially early fetuses, aren't capable of doing wrong, since they can't *intentionally* do anything, especially anything with moral dimensions. Fetuses seem to be neither innocent nor not: the concept just doesn't apply to them. (It's doubtful that animals can be *morally* blameworthy, but they are often called 'innocent' when they haven't done anything that's dangerous to others: this suggests that being capable of *doing* things is necessary for 'innocence').

Are fetuses "**vulnerable**"? Recall the image of animals in fear, trying to evade their killers. Imagine a child cowering in fear, covering her head to shield herself from blows from an abusive parent. These are paradigm instances of the abuse of a vulnerable being: they reveal vulnerability.

Are abortions like that? Are *early* abortions, of early fetuses, like that? More detailed information about the development of fetal consciousness and the potential for fetal pain will be given below, but at least early fetuses are not yet conscious and are not able to feel anything: their brains and nervous systems are not yet developed for that. Given what fetuses are like, at early stages, to call them "vulnerable" may be a stretch of the term: what are they vulnerable to? At least, they are very different from the clearly vulnerable animal or child examples above in that they physically and emotionally *experience* their abuse. Early fetuses don't experience anything, yet. So, while animals can be described as innocent and vulnerable, it is unclear that those concepts apply to early fetuses.

Some argue that fetuses are **persons** (from conception?) and so abortion is *prima facie* wrong. While persons *are* prima facie wrong to kill, we need to ask what is meant by 'person'. Some respond, 'human being,' which is not going to lead anywhere for animal rights. More thoughtful answers recognize that there are, or could be, divine persons and extra-terrestrial persons: in science fiction, humans interact with friendly and intelligent extra-terrestrials as their moral equals (as they would be). And a human body can remain biologically alive but the person gone: this is why being alive in a permanent coma is not much better than being dead, if that individual's consciousness will never return.

What are **persons**, then, on this account? Roughly, *beings with personalities*: conscious, feeling beings with abilities to perceive, reason (in some manner and at some level), have emotions, can communicate, a sense of self and so on. The idea is that personhood is determined by one's psychology and so personhood could, and perhaps does, emerge in bodies that are not human: if there is a God, personhood occurs in a being without a body at all.

This definition of personhood arguably applies to many animals: they have thoughts, feelings, memories, anticipations and unique personalities tying all these psychological states and abilities together. Are cats and dogs and cows and pigs more "like us," as persons, or are they more like carrots or rocks, clearly non-persons? If "like us," then perhaps they are closer to being persons than many suspected.

Whether this theory of personhood applies to fetuses, whether and when they are persons, depends on what they are like in terms of their cognitive, mental or psychological development. Here is some relevant information:

> • *Fetal consciousness and pain:* Most medical and scientific research finds that, at the earliest, <u>fetuses likely become conscious and develop an ability to feel pain around the end of the second or beginning of the third trimester of pregnancy</u>. (See also <u>here</u>, among many other sources). At least one philosopher, Cheryl Abbate, however, has argued that, to give fetuses every benefit of the doubt (such as the doubts given to think that some invertebrate animals feel pain), <u>fetuses might become conscious and able to feel pain at around 8 weeks.</u>[2]

> • *When Abortions Occur:* The CDC <u>reports</u>: "In 2012, the majority (65.8%) of abortions were performed by ≤8 weeks' gestation, and nearly all (91.4%) were performed by ≤13

weeks' gestation. Few abortions (7.2%) were performed between 14–20 weeks' gestation or at ≥21 weeks' gestation (1.3%)."

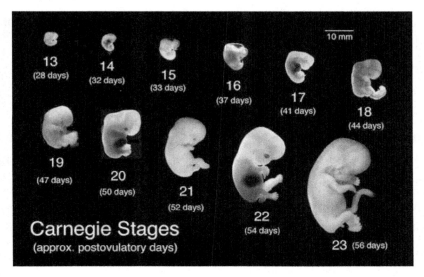

Source: Brad Smith
at http://embryo.soad.umich.edu/carnStages/carnStages.html

There is room for informed empirical debate these issues, and the CDC numbers are limited to the United States. But this information suggests that most aborted fetuses are, fortunately, not conscious and can't feel anything and that these fetuses are not **persons**, on a psychological definition. Early abortions involve killing **biologically human beings**, but not human persons: **potential persons** (discussed below), yes; **human organisms**, yes; beings of the "kind" *rational moral agent*, yes: but recall that these arguments don't apply to animals.

(Another view is that persons are *intrinsically valuable beings*. This is a fine answer, but we must ask who or what has that type of value and *why* – what *makes* a being have that type of value –

and that takes us back to the answers we are discussing here).

If fetuses aren't persons, they are *potential* **persons**, and that makes abortion wrong, some argue. Insofar as most animals whose rights in question are, arguably, already actual persons – on the psychological definition of personhood – that would imply that they are not potential persons: if you are actually something, you aren't potentially that same thing. So any proposal for how potential persons should be treated won't apply to actual persons: again, there's no connection. (The other premise of the argument though, that *potential persons have the rights of actual persons*, such as the right to life, is doubtful since *potential* beings [potential doctors, lawyers, presidents, parents, adults, spouses, senior citizens, and on] never have the rights of *actual* beings of that kind, in virtue of that potential. Arguments against abortion from potential personhood are doubtful).

Finally, some might respond that these above arguments evade the simple point that *abortions seriously* **harm** *fetuses*, and so abortions are wrong. Causing serious harms is *prima facie* wrong, and animals clearly can be (and are) harmed: the idea of cruelty to animals and calls for the "humane" treatment of animals presume that animals can be harmed, and that certain harms must be minimized. So this type of argument connects the issues.

But are early, pre-conscious fetuses harmed when aborted? Some might quickly react that they are *obviously* are, since they are destroyed and killed. Thinking through the nature of "harm" though suggests perhaps otherwise. Think about all the ways you can be harmed: physically, emotionally, cognitively, financially, and more. In each case, you are always made worse off, in some important way, *compared to how you were*: something happened and now, from your perspective, you are worse off. This suggests that to be harmed, one needs a perspective that can take a turn for the worse. But pre-conscious fetuses have no perspective: they are not aware of anything, yet. So, it seems that they cannot be made worse off, compared to how they were, since they never "were" in a conscious way. Later conscious and feeling fetuses can be harmed, but not early fetuses, it seems.

In reply, it must be observed that abortion usually results in a **future person** not being born: because of an abortion, there is some future individual who does not exist. While that's true, it is surely not wrong to not reproduce and contraception, including by abstinence, prevents the existence of future people. But we don't usually think of that as harmful: who would it harm? Someone who doesn't yet exist? Since it's not wrong to *not* bring future people into the world, that abortion has this same result wouldn't make it wrong either.

To conclude, these are a few common arguments that abortion is wrong. Some of these arguments don't connect to animal rights: **human–** and **moral agent**-based arguments, at least. Arguments from **innocence** and **vulnerability** and psychological **personhood** might support animal rights. But we saw that these may not be very strong arguments about abortion, at least early abortions, since these early fetuses might not really be innocent, or vulnerable or persons, given what they are like and the nature of these concepts. These doubtful arguments about abortion might support animal rights though, nevertheless.

These are just a few arguments about abortion though, quickly discussed, and none of them were theological or religious-based. Further arguments could, and should, be investigated to seek connections from anti-abortion arguments to pro-animal arguments: maybe a strong argument would be found that connects the issues.

3. Animal Rights?

Now let's go the other direction and consider some arguments about animal rights to see if they lead us to think that abortion is wrong.

Cases for **moral rights** for animals or, more generally, views that *it is wrong to seriously harm animals for food, experimentation, entertainment and other purposes* – this this view can be stated without mentioning 'rights' – depend on the observation that many animals have minds: they are conscious, are aware, and can feel pain and can suffer. This is true of mammals and birds, likely all vertebrates (including fish) and perhaps some invertebrates also. These animals also have positive feelings: pleasure, happiness and other positive emotions. And they are not disconnected blips of consciousness: they are psychologically unified by memories, anticipations, knowledge, social relationships and distinct personalities. They are individuals: each is a someone not a something.

Combine those facts about animals' minds with many plausible moral theories or principles and we are on our way to an animal-rights-like view. That theory might be utilitarian-related and concerned with the **pleasures and pains** of *all* beings who can experience such feelings, not just humans. Or it might be Kantian and emphasize treating *all* conscious beings as **ends-in-themselves**, not just rational beings. Or it might, as a **Golden Rule** and **John Rawls** require, demand that we treat others in ways we would be willing to be treated, seeing things from their perspectives as best we can. There are many moral-theoretical options to justify the belief that conscious animals have basic rights to avoiding pain and suffering, rights from other types of harms and, most importantly, rights to their own bodies and lives.

4. Animal Rights and Early Fetuses' Rights?

Our purpose here isn't to defend animal rights though. It's to see what animal-rights arguments imply or suggest for human fetuses and abortion. Is there a connection?

Not really.

Animal rights principles apply to **conscious, feeling beings – sentient beings** – and early, first trimester fetuses are not that. According to the information above about fetal consciousness and when most abortions occur, most aborted fetuses are not yet conscious and so can't feel anything.

So should animal rights advocates oppose early abortions? Not for any *plausible* reasons they give to think that animals have rights, since those reasons just don't apply to early fetuses. If someone thought that animals have rights because they are "life," as we saw above, this implies that vegetables and plants and mold and bacteria have rights, a conclusion that animal advocates and anyone else sensibly rejects. So, if and when animal rights advocates are pro-life about early abortions, it wouldn't be for animal-rights or, more generally, *conscious-or-sentient-being-rights-*related reasons: it'd have to be another argument.

Some mistakenly argue that animal rights arguments positively imply that fetuses lack rights. They offer this charge against animal rights advocates:

> You think that if a being is conscious and feeling, then it has rights. But you say early fetuses are not conscious and feeling. So you must think that they don't have rights.

But this argument is logically invalid, "denying the antecedent," just like this argument:

> You think that if Eve goes to State College, then Eve is a college student. But you know that Eve doesn't go to State College. Therefore, you must think Eve is not a college student.

Since Eve could attend a private college, that means the premises could be true but the conclusion false. So, these premises do not lead to the conclusion or justify it, and this pattern of reasoning is never good.

In sum, plausible animal rights arguments don't justify thinking that early fetuses have rights or, importantly, that they lack rights: they are neutral on the issue and so further arguments are needed to go either way on abortion, pro-choice or pro-life.

5. Animal Rights and Later Fetuses' Rights?

Later abortions, affecting **conscious and feeling** fetuses, are a different issue, however.

Obviously we don't know what it's like to be a fetus, but being killed in an abortion would surely feel horrific, to say the least. According to moral principles that motivate animal rights, causing this type of **pain** would surely be wrong unless done for a very good reason, and so animal rights-related thinking seems to reject any possible pro-choice views that claim that abortions are nearly necessarily morally permissible, that an abortion just could never be morally wrong, even if done very late in pregnancy and for frivolous reasons.

What might a good reason be to painfully abort a conscious, feeling fetus? At least, if this type of abortion was required to save the pregnant woman's life or prevent other harms to her *as bad or worse than the harms to the fetus from this type of abortion*, then that would be a good reason, it seems.

Fortunately, the numbers above suggest that relatively few abortions are of conscious, sentient fetuses: just a small percentage, perhaps a bit more if fetal consciousness develops earlier. These abortions are often performed because of serious disabilities found in the fetus: it is doubtful that women have later abortions for anything other than serious reasons. Regardless, the frequency of these later abortions could surely be reduced if early abortions were more readily available.

What else might be a good reason to potentially justify a later term abortion? Or *who* else?

Absent from our discussion so far has been the **pregnant woman**: she tends to be overlooked by anti-abortion arguments, which have been our focus. Obviously though, the fetus is developing in her body and will be making major demands on her and her body over pregnancy and birth.

Would a fetus have a *right* to her body, especially if that fetus was conscious and feeling? Philosopher Judith Thompson, in her famous 1971 "A Defense of Abortion" article, observed that other people don't rights to our bodies, even if they need our bodies to stay alive: you don't have a right to my kidney, even if you need it to live, and I don't violate your rights if you die because I don't give it to you. Fetuses, even if they were persons with the right to life, might not have a right to pregnant women's bodies, and pregnant women have a right to not allow fetuses to use their bodies. This fact complicates later abortions and simplifies earlier ones: the emergence of fetal consciousness doesn't make later abortions straightforwardly wrong, and women's rights to their bodies makes early abortions more easily permissible.

It's useful here to compare animal and fetal rights. It's easy to respect animals' rights: just don't shoot them to hang their heads on the wall, don't electrocute them to turn them into fur coats, don't infect them with diseases, don't kill them to eat them. Animals' rights, mainly, are negative rights: basically, just leave them alone. Fetuses' rights, in contrast, would be positive rights: rights to various benefits and forms of assistance from the women they are inside of. A pregnant woman surely does not just "leave the fetus alone" over the course of pregnancy and childbirth, so to speak: she has to put in a lot of physical and emotional effort and energy, to say the least. And a pregnant woman might not be willing, for many reasons, to provide those benefits to a fetus, given all that's involved. If Thompson is correct, the fetus has no right to these benefits, even if they are necessary for his or her life to continue, and the pregnant woman has a right to not provide them: until there are artificial wombs to transplant unwanted fetuses into, a woman has a moral right to an abortion.

These considerations about rights provide further reason to think that early abortions are morally permissible, beyond the inability of the above arguments to show that early abortions are wrong. It also provides another reason to think that later abortions, even of conscious and feeling fetuses, could be morally permissible. But we need to be cautious here: again, even if you need my kidney to stay alive, I have a right to my kidney. If, however, somehow you need my kidney *to avoid being brutally tortured to death*, I may be morally obligated to give you my kidney, whether you have a right to it or not (and maybe you would?!). And so *if* any later abortions are like that, for feeling fetuses, concern for their pain and suffering – if it is present – might trump a woman's rights here. The best response about this concern seems to be to ensure that this conflict of rights doesn't arise, by ensuring that any abortions happen early in pregnancy, before fetuses are conscious and can feel pain. And it might prompt developing methods to ensure that any later abortions are painless.

In sum, animal rights principles don't condemn early abortions and they don't *necessarily* condemn later abortions either. The perspectives and rights of the pregnant woman make the issues complex in ways that we never see with animal rights issues: in thinking about animal farming and slaughter, or experimentation, we confront animals as individuals. When they are in pairs or groups, such as mother and offspring, there never is a conflict of rights or ideal outcomes: what's best for one is always best for all. Abortion is not like that, by design.

6. Anti-Animal Rights and Pro-Life?

To ensure that our discussion is complete, we shouldn't forget that there are animal rights advocates *and* animal rights critics. Do any of the critics' arguments have any implications for abortion?

Yes. Some arguments emphasize that animals don't contribute to **(human) culture**, lack **intellectual accomplishments** and don't comprehend **the idea of rights**, and these concerns seem applicable to human fetuses also. But since they also apply to many children and adults also, these are poor objections to animal rights.

A more challenging argument against animal rights that claims that that animals lack rights because they are not human and/or because they are not the "kind" of being that's a *rational moral agent*. These arguments' advocates don't seem to notice that these arguments seem to imply that fetuses have rights, insofar as they are human and the kind of being that's a rational moral agent. So, to avoid animal rights, some people embrace an argument that seems to have "pro-life" implications, which they don't realize. Most people don't think that to consistently avoid thinking that animals have rights, they *must* think that abortion is wrong. And they need not. That this objection to animal rights has this result shows that it is not a good objection to animal rights. (This argument is developed in my "<u>Tom Regan on 'Kind' Arguments against Animal Rights and for Human Rights</u>" in *The Moral Rights of Animals*).

There may be other connections, but I will leave it to critics of animal rights to see what other implications their arguments might have for abortion.

7. Pro-Choice and Animal Rights?

Finally, do any of the reasons given to be pro-choice imply anything positive for animals?

There are many types of reasons to think that abortion is not wrong and many of them have no implications for animals: for examples, arguments that abortion is not wrong because fetuses are **not human beings** or **not conscious** or that they are **not**

persons have no implications for animals. Arguing that early fetuses lack the right to life because they don't have **any desires for the future** won't clearly apply to animals since they have some present desires that drift into the future. So some pro-choice arguments don't have any implications for animals.

Arguments for abortion based on women's rights, discussed above, suggest profound implications for animals, however. These arguments recognize that **pregnancy, childbirth and parenthood** are unique and profound experiences for nearly all women who experience them. Even when wanted, these are physically and emotionally challenging, life-altering events. And these aren't just things that happen, passively, to a woman: she is actively engaged in making them; she is part of them and they become her and she will never be the same.

Female animals who are mothers very likely have *some* similar experiences and feelings. There are obviously very important differences in the experiences of human and non-human mothers, but the simple and clear point is this: *animal mothers love their babies.* Cows used in dairy production (female, obviously) clearly grieve when their calves are forcibly taken from them so that they don't drink their own mother's milk, biologically meant for them: this is kidnapping and theft, so human beings can drink that calves' milk. And a "mother hen" is not just some made up phrase: she cares for her chicks, and they care for her. Animals change when they have babies.

Pro-choice thinkers emphasize that it should be a woman's **choice** to have maternal experiences, that whether she has these experiences should be under her **control**. This control includes the choice to not have these experiences (at least at this time, in this situation) and so abortion should be allowed, they argue. This impulse for reproductive and maternal control should, arguably, extend to female animals used in, for examples, the dairy and egg industries and some animal research. Female animals used in industries are typically forcibly impregnated. Dairy cows lose their calves and will fight to keep them. Hens don't get to nest with their eggs; they don't get to see their eggs hatch; they don't get to watch over their chicks. Some scientific research disrupts mother and offspring relations: remember Harlow's monkeys?

Female animals and their offspring endure many unique and specific harms in virtue of being female. Their reproduction and maternal experience is controlled by human choices which result in bad experiences and outcomes for animal mothers and their offspring. A certain type of **feminist thinking** about abortion should lead to an animal rights-like view, initially about certain harms to female animals. **Fairness and empathy** should then lead to concerns for any conscious and feeling animals, female or male: that is, unless there is some relevant difference here that would justify discrimination against female animals which, of course,

there isn't. And one hopes that people opposed
to **discrimination** against women and girls would be opposed
to **unfair** discrimination wherever it is found, whether its victims
are human or non-human, female or male, mother or child.

8. Conclusion

In sum, we have discussed two controversial issues: abortion and
animal rights. Not all issues are controversial though: it is
uncontroversial that it is *prima facie* wrong to kill human beings. If
asked why this is so, however, many would quickly respond,
"Because they are human!" But this answer takes us back to
controversies, since (biologically) human fetuses *are* human and it's
debatable whether it's wrong to kill them, and non-human animals
are clearly *not* human and it's debatable whether it is wrong to kill
them also. '**Human**' then, seems to not be much of a moral
explanation.

Here we have explored some potentially deeper explanations
about each topic, some more sophisticated arguments, trying to
see if any reasons given in favor of views on one topic clearly
extend to the other topic. Generally, with a few exceptions, they
don't. That means that one's views about one topic generally
needn't be *determined* by one's views about the other. Even when
some connections or implications are suggested, there are ways to
avoid these suggestions, given the differences between the issues.
Whether all those ways of resisting a suggested implication of
one's moral principles are rational or intellectually responsible, we
would have to see. By developing our skills at doing just that
would surely improve our skills at theorizing and arguing about
both animal rights and abortion and continuing to try to discern
what to think about these issues individually, in relation to each

other and, potentially, in relation to other pressing ethical and social issues.[3]

NOTES

[1] For arguments that pro-lifers should accept animal rights, see, e.g., Matthew Scully, "Pro-Life, Pro-Animal," *The National Review*, October 7, 2013 and an interview with Charles Camosy, "Should Every Pro-lifer be a Vegetarian?" *National Review Interviews*, October 21, 2013. For arguments that animal rights advocates, or vegetarians, should be pro-life, see, e.g., Mary Eberstadt, "Pro-Animal, Pro-Life," *First Things* 194 (2009): 15. Charles Camosy suggests that the values supporting pro-life and animal rights positions are similar or shared in "Outraged over Cecil the lion? It may help you understand the rage over Planned Parenthood," *LA Times*, July 30, 2015. For further discussion, including of feminist arguments concerning both abortion and animal rights, see Abbate, C. E. (2015), "Adventures in Moral Consistency: How to Develop an Abortion Ethic through an Animal Rights Framework," *Ethical Theory and Moral Practice*, *18*(1), 145-164; Jenni, K. (1994), "Dilemmas in social philosophy: abortion and animal rights," *Social Theory and Practice*, *20*(1), 59-83; and Colb, S., & Dorf, M. (2016), *Beating Hearts: Abortion and Animal Rights*, Columbia University Press. See my 6/25/16 review of Colb and Dorf at *Notre Dame Philosophy Reviews* at https://ndpr.nd.edu/news/67959-beating-hearts-abortion-and-animal-rights/which inspired this essay.

[2] See Lee, S. J., Ralston, H. J. P., Drey, E. A., Partridge, J. C., & Rosen, M. A. (2005). "Fetal Pain: A Systematic Multidisciplinary Review of the Evidence," *Jama*, *294*(8), 947-954; Benatar, D. and Benatar, M. (2001), "A Pain in the Fetus: Toward Ending

Confusion about Fetal Pain," *Bioethics*, 15: 57–76. doi: 10.1111/1467-8519.00212; and Abbate, C. E. (2015), "Adventures in Moral Consistency: How to Develop an Abortion Ethic through an Animal Rights Framework," *Ethical Theory and Moral Practice*, *18*(1), 145-164

[3] Sources for open access images: garden:https://upload.wikimedia.org/wikipedia/commons/7/7d/Raised_bed.jpg; moldy fruit:https://upload.wikimedia.org/wikipedia/commons/6/6e/Moldy_nectarines.jpg; mosquito:https://upload.wikimedia.org/wikipedia/commons/e/ea/Aedes_Albopictus.jpg; human blood cells:https://upload.wikimedia.org/wikipedia/commons/5/56/Agarplate_redbloodcells_edit.jpg; embryo development:https://upload.wikimedia.org/wikipedia/commons/thumb/0/08/Haeckel_drawings.jpg/350px-Haeckel_drawings.jpg;Carnegie stages:**Brad Smith** at http://embryo.soad.umich.edu/carnStages/carnStages.html ; cow with calf:https://upload.wikimedia.org/wikipedia/commons/f/fb/New_born_Frisian_red_white_calf.jpg; hen with chicks: https://pixabay.com/en/chicks-yellow-mother-hen-hen-1433003/

ABOUT THE AUTHOR

Nathan Nobis, Ph.D. is an Associate Professor of Philosophy at Morehouse College, Atlanta, GA. He has taught courses, given Chapters and published articles and chapters on a wide variety of topics concerning ethics and animals, bioethics, ethical theory and other topics in philosophy. His webpage is at NathanNobis.com

CPSIA information can be obtained
at www.ICGtesting.com
Printed in the USA
LVOW13s1134260217
525458LV00010B/889/P